MAGELLAN GEOGRAPHIX

WORLD HISTORY ATLAS

Contents

©2000 Maps.com / MAGELLAN Geographix, 6464 Hollister Avenue, Santa Barbara, CA 93117 / 800-929-4MAP / 805-685-3100.

Visit the world's premier map website at **http://www.maps.com** — thousands of quality map products and services for purchase. Map viewing, driving directions and an address finder are available free of charge. For additional educational map collections and resources, visit **http://www.maps101.com**.

Cover art: World map by Frederick deWit, 1660. Image from a digital collection of antique maps by Visual Language Library.

ISBN 1-930194-00-5

EARLY CIVILIZATIONS, c. 8000–900 BCE

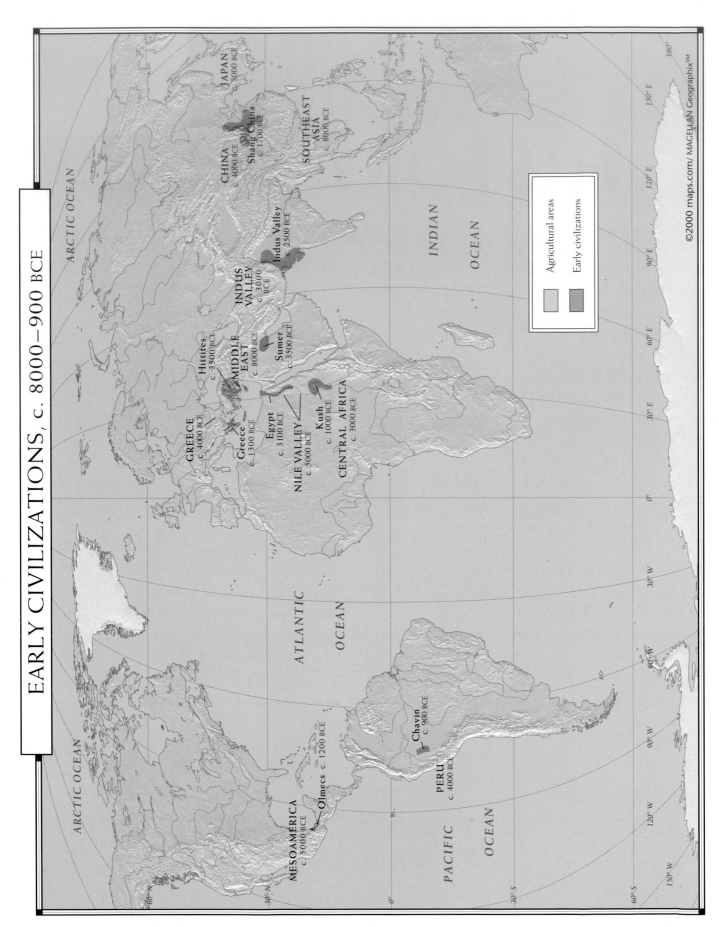

ARCTIC OCEAN

JAPAN
c. 3000 BCE

CHINA
c. 4000 BCE

Shang China
c. 1700 BCE

SOUTHEAST
ASIA
c. 8000 BCE

Indus Valley
c. 2500 BCE

INDUS
VALLEY
c. 3000
BCE

INDIAN

OCEAN

Hittites
c. 3500 BCE

MIDDLE
EAST
c. 8000 BCE

Sumer
c. 3500 BCE

GREECE
c. 4000 BCE

Greece
c. 1300 BCE

Egypt
c. 3100 BCE

NILE VALLEY
c. 5000 BCE

Kush
c. 1000 BCE

CENTRAL AFRICA
c. 3000 BCE

ATLANTIC

OCEAN

Chavin
c. 900 BCE

PERU
c. 4000 BCE

MESOAMERICA
c. 5000 BCE

Olmecs c. 1200 BCE

PACIFIC

OCEAN

ARCTIC OCEAN

Agricultural areas

Early civilizations

©2000 maps.com / MAGELLAN Geographix℠

THE SPREAD OF AGRICULTURE, c. 10,000–1000 BCE

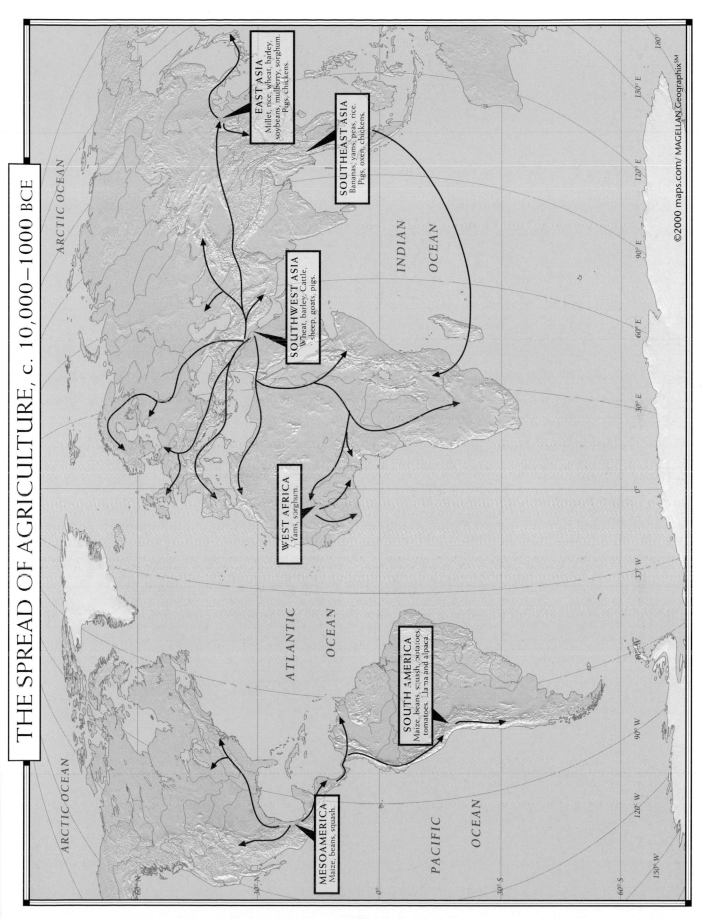

EAST ASIA
Millet, rice, wheat, barley, soybeans, mulberry, sorghum. Pigs, chickens.

SOUTHEAST ASIA
Bananas, yams, peas, rice. Pigs, oxen, chickens.

SOUTHWEST ASIA
Wheat, barley. Cattle, sheep, goats, pigs.

WEST AFRICA
Yams, sorghum.

SOUTH AMERICA
Maize, beans, squash, potatoes, tomatoes. Llama and alpaca.

MESOAMERICA
Maize, beans, squash.

ARCTIC OCEAN

ARCTIC OCEAN

INDIAN OCEAN

ATLANTIC OCEAN

PACIFIC OCEAN

©2000 maps.com/ MAGELLAN Geographix℠

MESOPOTAMIA AND EGYPT, c. 4000 BCE – 1000 BCE

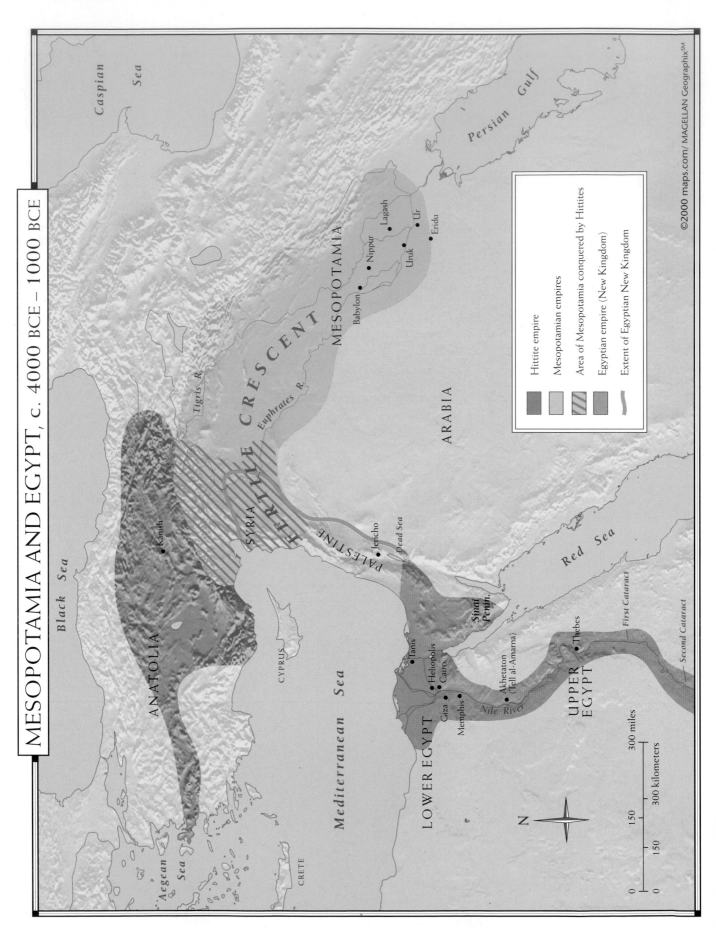

©2000 maps.com/ MAGELLAN Geographix℠

Caspian Sea

Black Sea

Persian Gulf

Tigris R.

Euphrates R.

FERTILE CRESCENT

MESOPOTAMIA

Lagash
Nippur
Babylon
Uruk
Ur
Eridu

ARABIA

SYRIA

PALESTINE

Jericho
Dead Sea

Red Sea

Kanish

ANATOLIA

CYPRUS

Mediterranean Sea

Aegean Sea

CRETE

Sinai Penin.

Tanis
Heliopolis
Cairo
Giza
Memphis
Akhetaton
(Tell al-Amarna)
Nile River

Thebes

First Cataract

Second Cataract

LOWER EGYPT

UPPER EGYPT

N

Legend
- Hittite empire
- Mesopotamian empires
- Area of Mesopotamia conquered by Hittites
- Egyptian empire (New Kingdom)
- Extent of Egyptian New Kingdom

0   150   300 miles
0   150   300 kilometers

INDO-EUROPEAN MIGRATIONS, c. 4000 BCE–1000 BCE

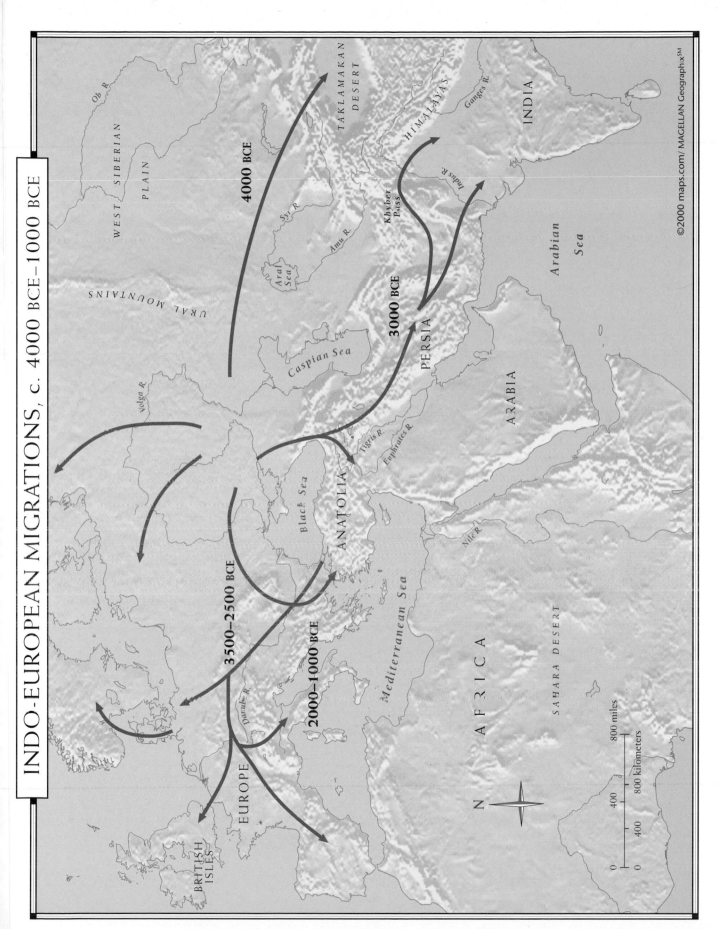

©2000 maps.com/ MAGELLAN Geographix℠

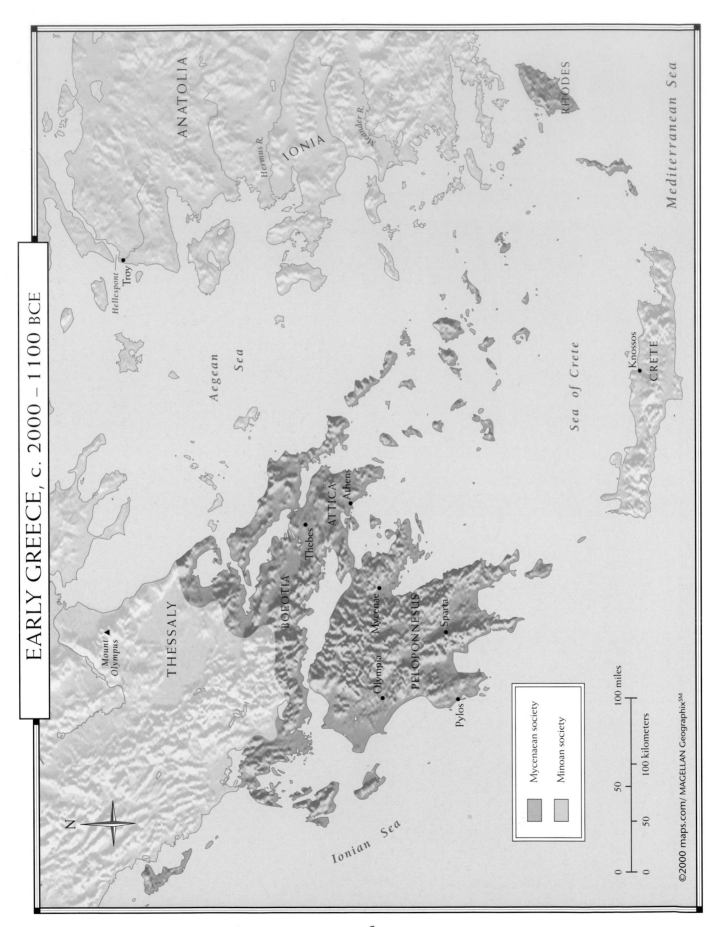

EARLY GREECE, c. 2000 – 1100 BCE

ANATOLIA

IONIA

Hermus R.

Meander R.

RHODES

Mediterranean Sea

Hellespont

Troy

Aegean Sea

Sea of Crete

Knossos

CRETE

THESSALY

Mount Olympus

BOEOTIA

Thebes

ATTICA

Athens

Mycenae

Sparta

PELOPONNESUS

Olympia

Pylos

Ionian Sea

N

Mycenaean society

Minoan society

100 miles

100 kilometers

50

50

0

0

©2000 maps.com/ MAGELLAN Geographix℠

THE SPREAD OF WORLD RELIGIONS, c. 500 BCE–600 CE

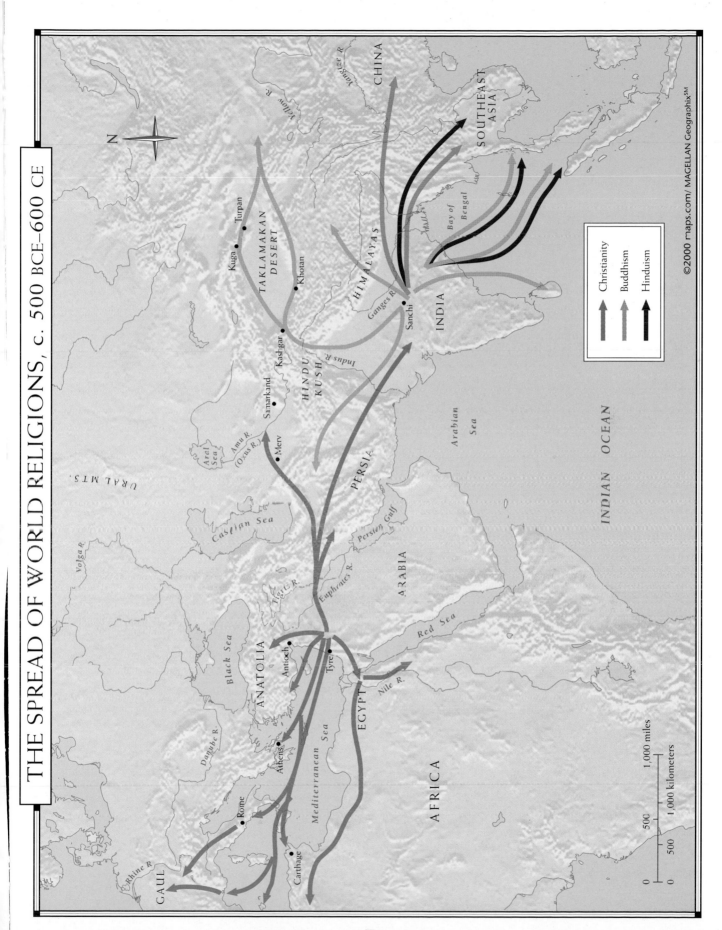

©2000 maps.com / MAGELLAN Geographix℠

Christianity

Buddhism

Hinduism

N

CHINA

SOUTHEAST ASIA

Yangzi R.

Yellow R.

Bay of Bengal

TAKLAMAKAN DESERT

Turpan

Kuqa

Khotan

HIMALAYAS

Ganges R.

Sanchi

INDIA

HINDU KUSH

Indus R.

Kashgar

Samarkand

Amu R. (Oxus R.)

Aral Sea

Merv

URAL MTS.

Arabian Sea

INDIAN OCEAN

PERSIA

Caspian Sea

Volga R.

Tigris R.

Euphrates R.

Persian Gulf

ARABIA

Red Sea

Black Sea

ANATOLIA

Antioch

Tyre

Nile R.

EGYPT

Athens

Mediterranean Sea

AFRICA

Rome

Danube R.

Carthage

Rhine R.

GAUL

1,000 miles

1,000 kilometers

500

500

0

0

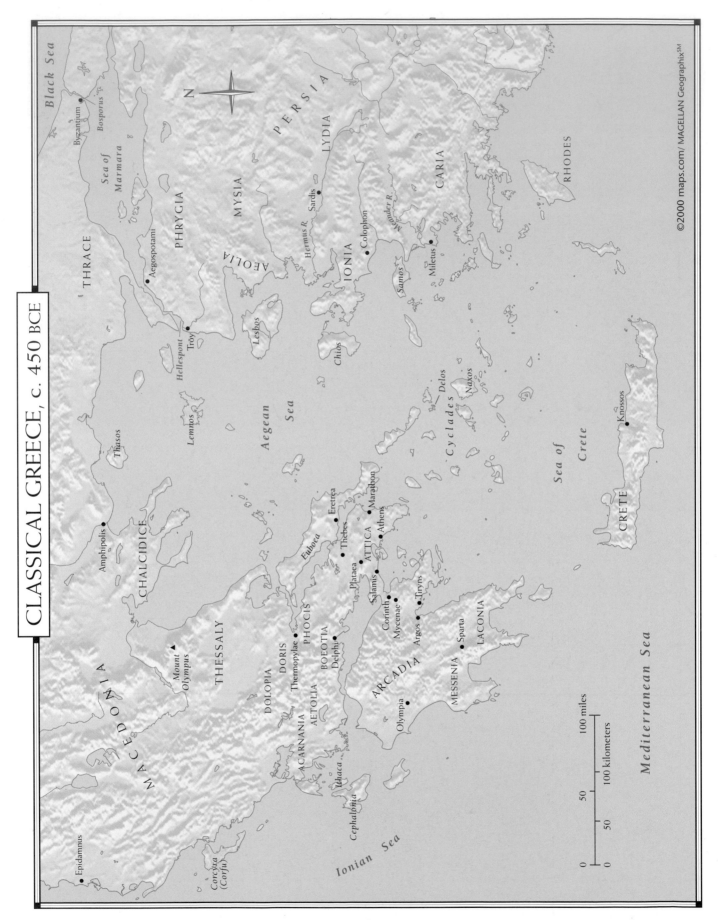

CLASSICAL GREECE, c. 450 BCE

©2000 maps.com/ MAGELLAN Geographix℠

Black Sea

Byzantium

Bosporus

Sea of Marmara

THRACE

PHRYGIA

MYSIA

AEOLIA

PERSIA

LYDIA

Sardis

Hermus R.

IONIA

Colophon

Maeander R.

Samos

Miletus

CARIA

RHODES

Aegospotami

Hellespont

Troy

Lesbos

Chios

Thasos

Lemnos

Aegean Sea

Cyclades

Delos

Naxos

Sea of Crete

Knossos

CRETE

CRETE

Amphipolis

CHALCIDICE

MACEDONIA

Mount Olympus

THESSALY

DOLOPIA

DORIS

Thermopylae

PHOCIS

AETOLIA

ACARNANIA

Delphi

BOEOTIA

Euboea

Eretrea

Thebes

Plataea

Salamis

ATTICA

Marathon

Athens

Corinth

Mycenae

Argos

Tiryns

ARCADIA

Olympia

MESSENIA

Sparta

LACONIA

Ithaca

Cephalonia

Corcyra (Corfu)

Ionian Sea

Epidamnus

Mediterranean Sea

100 miles

100 kilometers

50

50

0

0

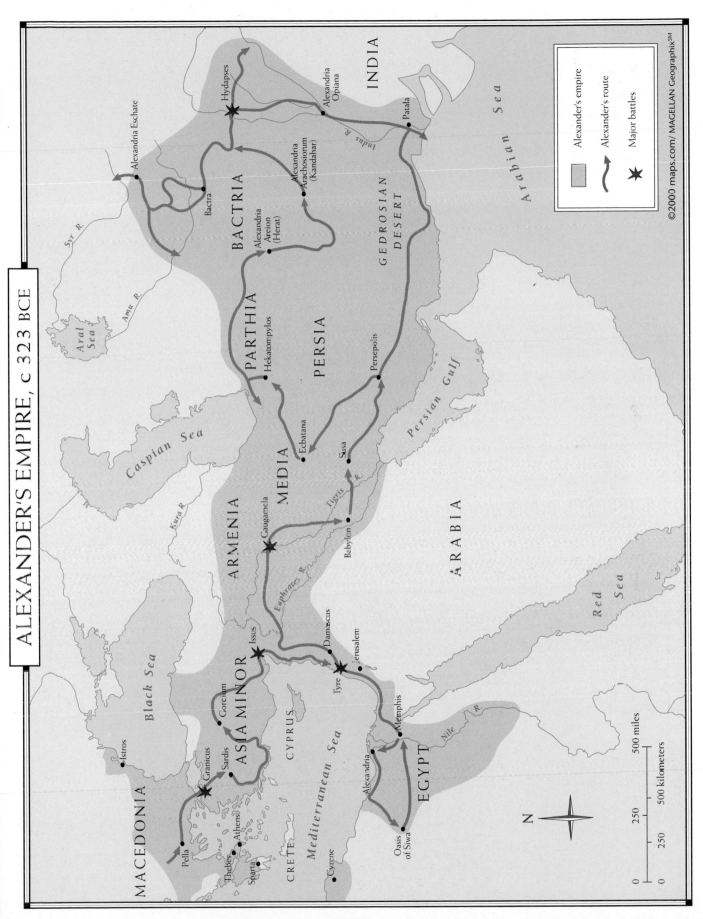

ALEXANDER'S EMPIRE, c 323 BCE

©2000 maps.com/ MAGELLAN Geographix℠

Alexander's empire

Alexander's route

Major battles

INDIA

Alexandria Eschate

Hydaspes

Alexandria Opiana

Patala

BACTRIA

Bactra

Alexandria Arachosiorum (Kandahar)

PARTHIA

Alexandria Areion (Herat)

GEDROSIAN DESERT

Indus R.

Arabian Sea

Aral Sea

Syr R.

Amu R.

Hekatompylos

PERSIA

Persepolis

Persian Gulf

Caspian Sea

Ecbatana

Susa

Babylon

Tigris

Euphrates

Kura R.

ARMENIA

MEDIA

Gaugamela

ARABIA

Red Sea

Black Sea

Istros

Granicus

Sardis

Gordium

ASIA MINOR

CYPRUS

Issus

Damascus

Jerusalem

Tyre

Memphis

Alexandria

Nile R.

EGYPT

Oasis of Siwa

MACEDONIA

Pella

Thebes

Athens

Sparta

CRETE

Cyrene

Mediterranean Sea

N

500 miles

500 kilometers

0   250   500

0   250   500

-9-

MESOAMERICAN SOCIETIES, c. 1200 BCE–900 CE

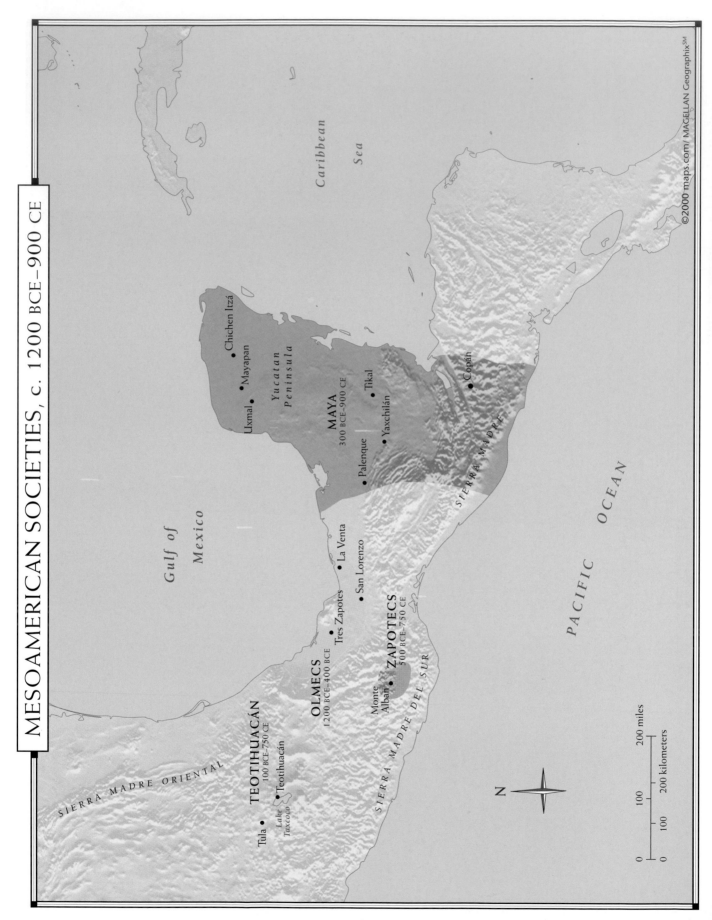

©2000 maps.com/ MAGELLAN Geographix℠

Caribbean Sea

Gulf of Mexico

Yucatan Peninsula

• Chichen Itzá

• Mayapán

Uxmal •

MAYA
300 BCE–900 CE

• Tikal

Palenque •

• Yaxchilán

• Copán

SIERRA MADRE

PACIFIC OCEAN

La Venta •

• San Lorenzo

Tres Zapotes •

OLMECS
1200 BCE–400 BCE

Monte
Albán •

ZAPOTECS
500 BCE–750 CE

SIERRA MADRE DEL SUR

TEOTIHUACÁN
100 BCE–750 CE

Tula •

Lake
Texcoco   • Teotihuacán

SIERRA MADRE ORIENTAL

N

0   100   200 miles

0   100   200 kilometers

THE ROMAN EMPIRE, 44 BCE – 117 CE

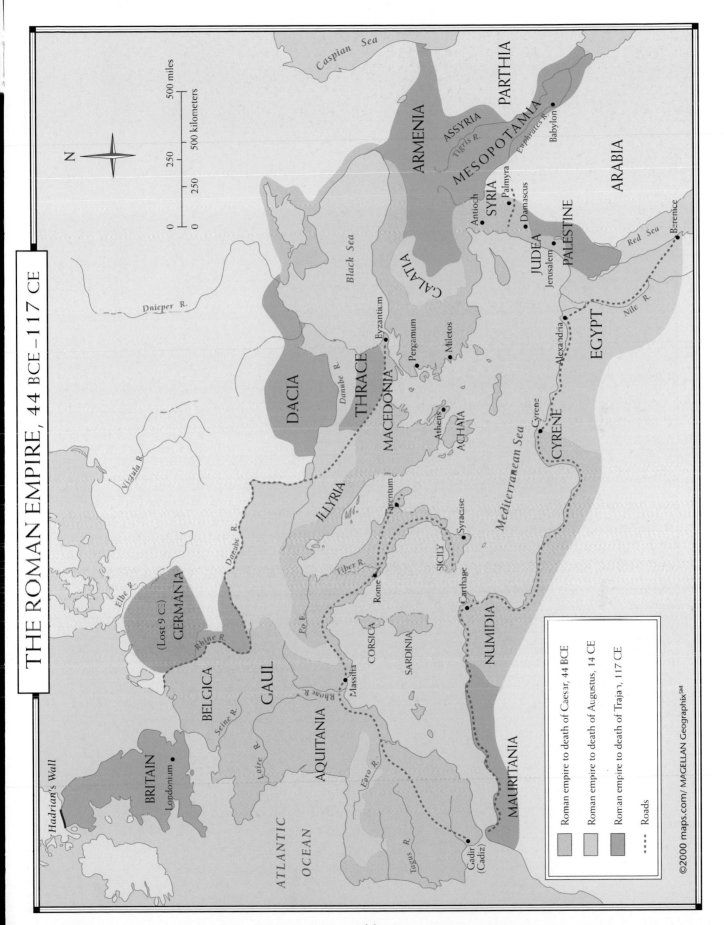

N

500 miles
500 kilometers
250
250
0
0

Caspian Sea

PARTHIA

ARMENIA

ASSYRIA

MESOPOTAMIA

Tigris R.

Euphrates R.

Babylon

ARABIA

Antioch
SYRIA
Palmyra
Damascus

PALESTINE

JUDEA

Jerusalem

Red Sea

Berenice

Nile R.

Alexandria

EGYPT

Black Sea

GALATIA

Dnieper R.

Pergamum

Miletos

Byzantium

Danube R.

DACIA

THRACE

MACEDONIA

Athens

ACHAIA

Cyrene

CYRENE

Mediterranean Sea

ILLYRIA

Tarentum

Syracuse

SICILY

Tiber R.

Rome

Po R.

CORSICA

SARDINIA

Carthage

NUMIDIA

MAURITANIA

Vistula R.

Elbe R.

Danube R.

GERMANIA
(Lost 9 CE)

Rhine R.

BELGICA

GAUL

Seine R.

AQUITANIA

Loire R.

Rhône R.

Massilia

Ebro R.

Tagus R.

Gadir
(Cadiz)

ATLANTIC
OCEAN

BRITAIN

Londonium

Hadrian's Wall

Roman empire to death of Caesar, 44 BCE

Roman empire to death of Augustus, 14 CE

Roman empire to death of Trajan, 117 CE

- - - - Roads

©2000 maps.com/ MAGELLAN Geographix℠

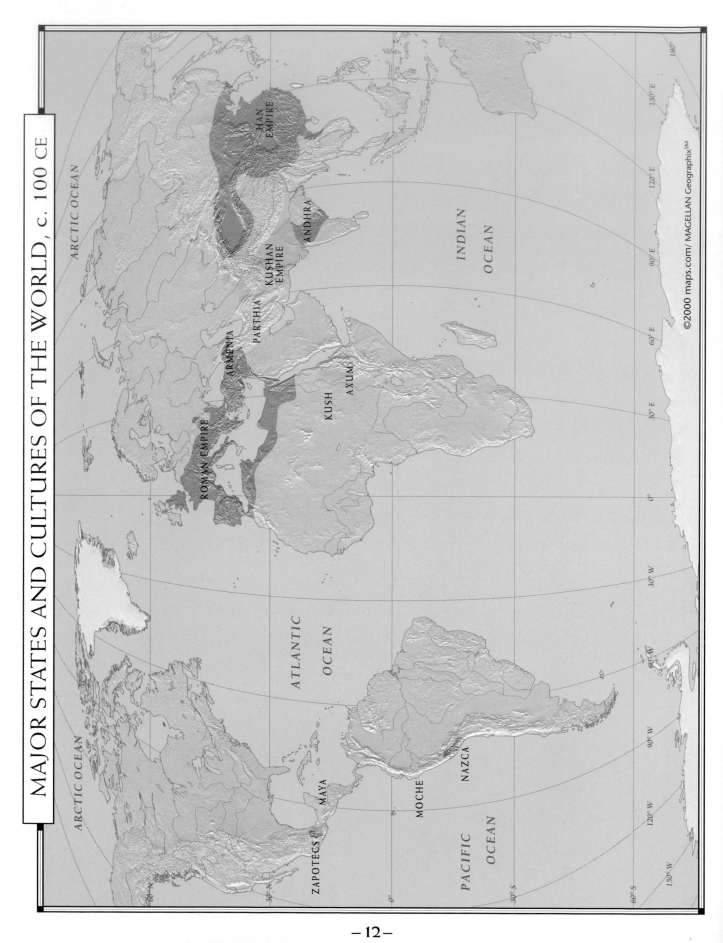

MAJOR STATES AND CULTURES OF THE WORLD, c. 100 CE

ARCTIC OCEAN

ARCTIC OCEAN

HAN EMPIRE

ANDHRA

KUSHAN EMPIRE

PARTHIA

ARMENIA

ROMAN EMPIRE

KUSH

AXUM

INDIAN OCEAN

ATLANTIC OCEAN

MAYA

ZAPOTECS

MOCHE

NAZCA

PACIFIC OCEAN

©2000 maps.com/ MAGELLAN Geographix℠

180°

130° E

120° E

90° E

60° E

30° E

0°

30° W

60° W

90° W

120° W

150° W

0°

30° S

60° S

30° N

THE ROMAN EMPIRE AND GERMANIC MIGRATIONS, c. 400 CE

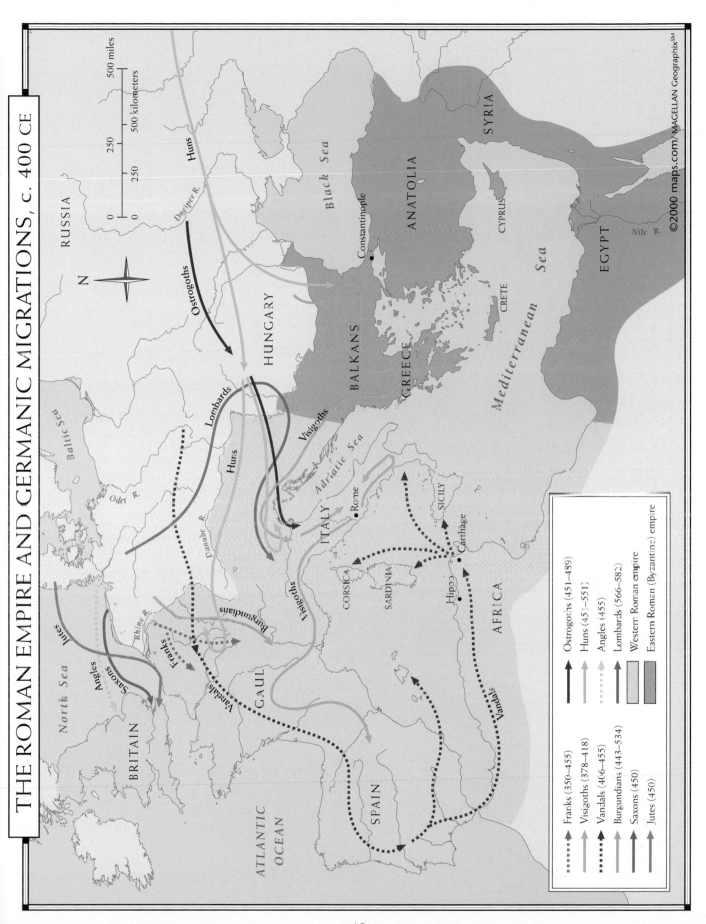

Legend:
- Franks (350–455)
- Visigoths (378–418)
- Vandals (406–455)
- Burgundians (443–534)
- Saxons (450)
- Jutes (450)
- Ostrogoths (451–489)
- Huns (451–551)
- Angles (455)
- Lombards (566–582)
- Western Roman empire
- Eastern Roman (Byzantine) empire

©2000 maps.com/ MAGELLAN Geographix℠

EUROPE AND THE BYZANTINE EMPIRE, 525–565 CE

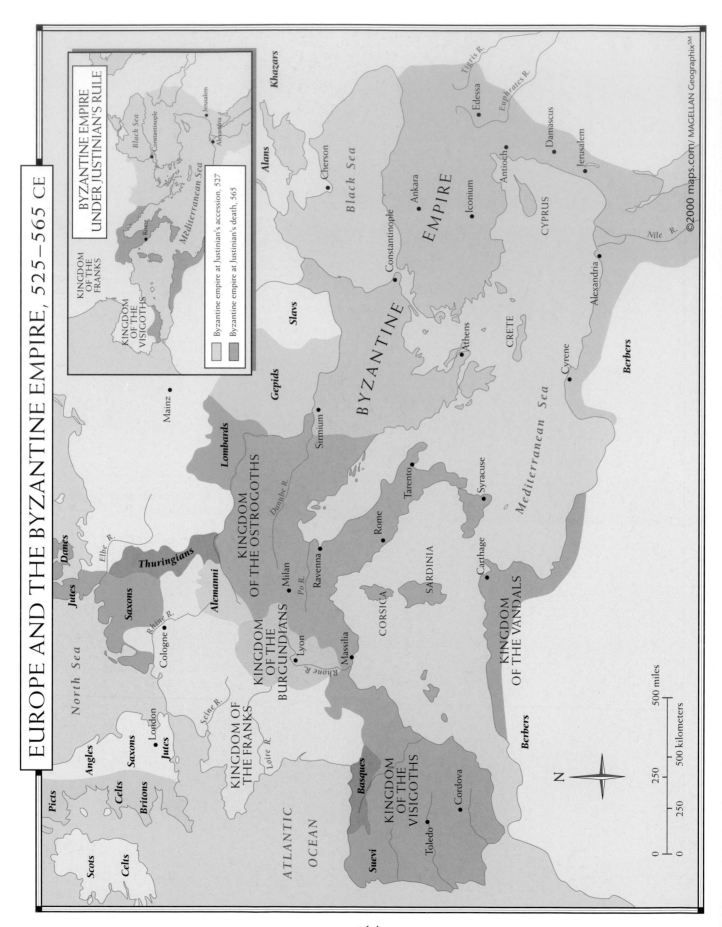

BYZANTINE EMPIRE
UNDER JUSTINIAN'S RULE

KINGDOM OF THE FRANKS

KINGDOM OF THE VISIGOTHS

Byzantine empire at Justinian's accession, 527

Byzantine empire at Justinian's death, 565

©2000 maps.com/ MAGELLAN Geographix℠

Khazars

Alans

Black Sea

Cherson

Slavs

Gepids

Constantinople

BYZANTINE EMPIRE

Ankara

Iconium

Antioch

Edessa

Damascus

Jerusalem

Tigris R.

Euphrates R.

CYPRUS

Nile R.

Alexandria

CRETE

Athens

Cyrene

Berbers

Mediterranean Sea

Mainz

Lombards

KINGDOM OF THE OSTROGOTHS

Danube R.

Sirmium

Milan

Po R.

Ravenna

Rome

Tarento

Syracuse

SARDINIA

Carthage

KINGDOM OF THE VANDALS

CORSICA

Massilia

Lyon

KINGDOM OF THE BURGUNDIANS

Rhône R.

Thuringians

Alemanni

Saxons

Jutes

Danes

Elbe R.

Rhine R.

Cologne

North Sea

Seine R.

London

Jutes

Saxons

Angles

KINGDOM OF THE FRANKS

Loire R.

Picts

Celts

Britons

Scots

Celts

ATLANTIC OCEAN

Basques

Suevi

KINGDOM OF THE VISIGOTHS

Toledo

Cordova

N

0   250   500 miles

0   250   500 kilometers

Inset map labels

Black Sea

Constantinople

Jerusalem

Alexandria

Mediterranean Sea

Rome

TRADE ROUTES IN THE INDIAN OCEAN, c. 500–1000 CE

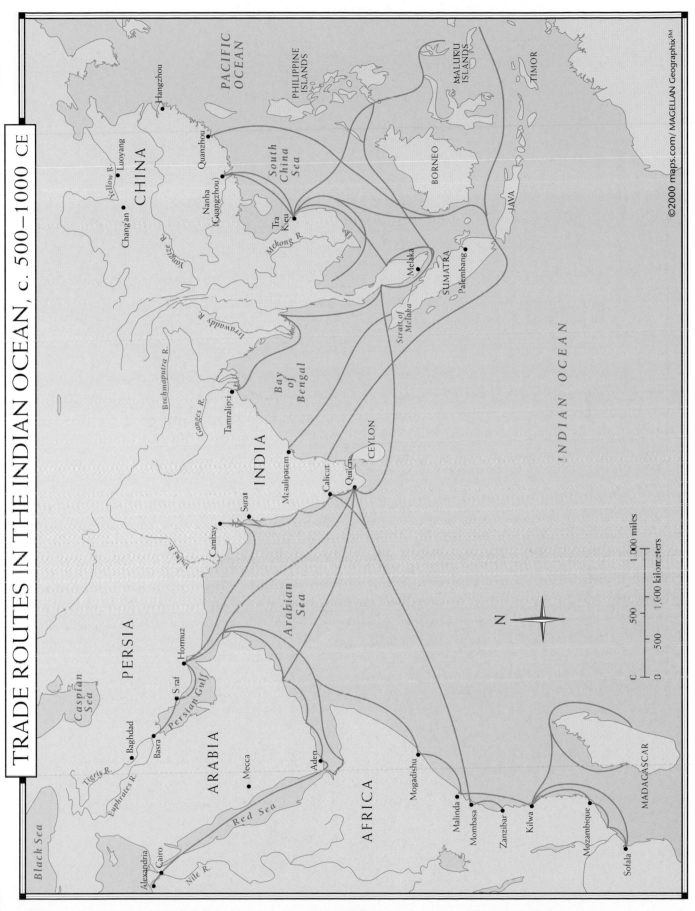

©2000 maps.com/ MAGELLAN Geographix℠

THE SPREAD OF ISLAM, 622 – 750 CE

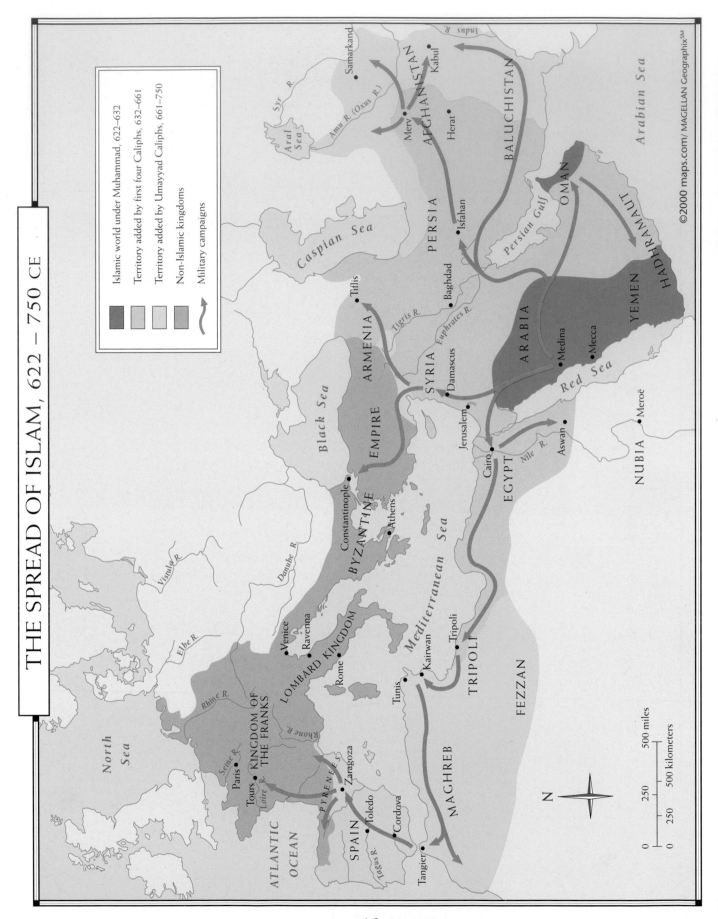

Legend:
- Islamic world under Muhammad, 622–632
- Territory added by first four Caliphs, 632–661
- Territory added by Umayyad Caliphs, 661–750
- Non-Islamic kingdoms
- Military campaigns

©2000 maps.com/ MAGELLAN Geographix℠

North Sea · ATLANTIC OCEAN · Elbe R. · Visula R. · Rhine R. · Danube R. · Seine R. · Loire R. · Rhone R. · Paris · Tours · KINGDOM OF THE FRANKS · PYRENEES · Zaragoza · SPAIN · Toledo · Cordova · Tagus R. · Tangier · MAGHREB · Venice · Ravenna · Rome · LOMBARD KINGDOM · Alps M. · Tunis · Kairwan · Tripoli · TRIPOLI · FEZZAN · Mediterranean Sea · BYZANTINE EMPIRE · Constantinople · Athens · Black Sea · Caspian Sea · ARMENIA · Tiflis · Aral Sea · Syr R. · Amu R. (Oxus R.) · Samarkand · Merv · AFGHANISTAN · Kabul · BALUCHISTAN · Herat · Indus R. · Arabian Sea · PERSIA · Isfahan · Baghdad · Tigris R. · Euphrates R. · SYRIA · Damascus · Jerusalem · Cairo · EGYPT · Nile R. · Aswan · NUBIA · Meroë · Red Sea · ARABIA · Medina · Mecca · YEMEN · HADHRAMAUT · OMAN · Persian Gulf

N

500 miles
500 kilometers
0   250   500
0   250   500

–16–

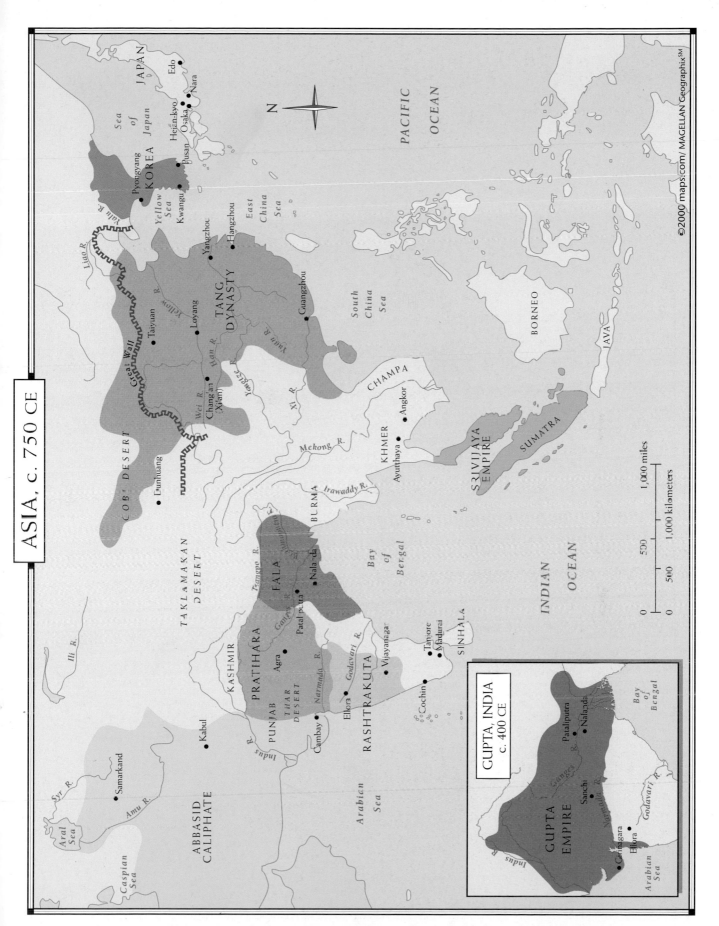

ASIA, c. 750 CE

JAPAN
Edo
Nara
Sea of Japan
Heian-kyo
Osaka
KOREA
Pusan
Pyongyang
Kwangu
Yellow Sea
Yangzhou
Hangzhou
East China Sea

PACIFIC OCEAN

©2000 maps.com/ MAGELLAN Geographix℠

Yalu R.
Liao R.
Great Wall
Taiyuan
Loyang
Yellow R.
Han R.
TANG DYNASTY
Guangzhou
Yangtze R.

GOBI DESERT
Dunhuang
Chang'an (Xi'an)
Wei R.
Xi R.
Yuan R.

South China Sea

BORNEO
JAVA

TAKLAMAKAN DESERT

CHAMPA
Angkor
KHMER
Ayutthaya

SRIVIJAYA EMPIRE
SUMATRA

Mekong R.
Irawaddy R.
BURMA

Bay of Bengal

INDIAN OCEAN

Ili R.

PALA
Tsangpo R.
Nala-da
Patal puta
Ganges R.
PRATIHARA
Agra
KASHMIR
THAR DESERT
Narmada R.
Godavari R.
PUNJAB
Ellora
Cambay
RASHTRAKUTA
Cochin
Vijayanaga
Tanjore
Madurai
SINHALA
Indus R.

Kabul

Samarkand
Syr R.
Amu R.
Aral Sea
Caspian Sea

ABBASID CALIPHATE

Arabian Sea

1,000 miles
500
1,000 kilometers
500
0
0

GUPTA, INDIA
c. 400 CE

GUPTA EMPIRE
Pataliputra
Nalanda
Ganges R.
Sanchi
Narmada R.
Godavari R.
Ellora
Girinagara
Indus R.
Arabian Sea
Bay of Bengal

–17–

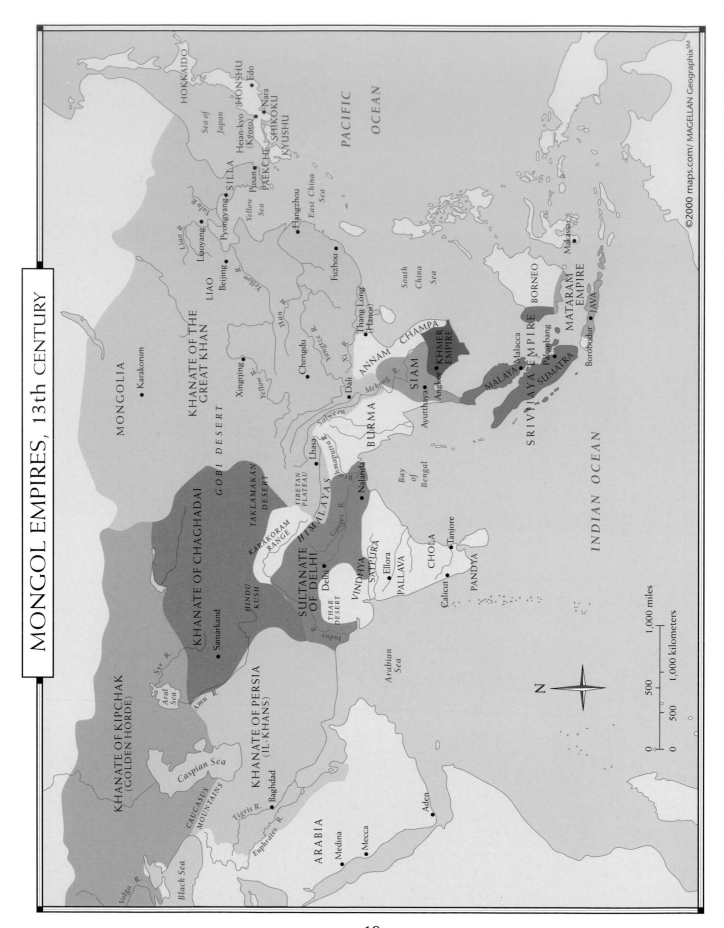

MONGOL EMPIRES, 13th CENTURY

©2000 maps.com/ MAGELLAN Geographix℠

MONGOLIA

Karakorum

KHANATE OF THE GREAT KHAN

GOBI DESERT

HOKKAIDO

HONSHU
Edo
Nara
Heian-kyo (Kyoto)
SHIKOKU
KYUSHU

Sea of Japan

PACIFIC OCEAN

SILLA
Pusan
PAEKCHE
Pyongyang

Yellow Sea

Liao R.
Laoyang
Beijing
LIAO

Liao R.
Yellow R.
Han R.

Hangzhou
Fuzhou

East China Sea

Yellow R.

Xingqing
Chengdu
Yangtze R.
Dali
Xi R.

Thang Long (Hanoi)

South China Sea

TAKLAMAKAN DESERT

KHANATE OF CHAGHADAI

TIBETAN PLATEAU
Lhasa

KARAKORAM RANGE

HIMALAYAS

Brahmaputra R.

Salween

Mekong R.

CHAMPA

ANNAM

SIAM
Ayutthaya

KHMER EMPIRE
Angkor

BURMA

MALAYA
Malacca

BORNEO

SRIVIJAYA EMPIRE
Palembang
SUMATRA

MATARAM EMPIRE
JAVA
Borobodur

Makassar

Samarkand

HINDU KUSH

SULTANATE OF DELHI
Delhi

Nalanda

Ganges R.

VINDHYA

SATPURA

Ellora
PALLAVA

CHOLA
Tanjore

PANDYA

Calicut

Bay of Bengal

INDIAN OCEAN

THAR DESERT

Indus

KHANATE OF KIPCHAK (GOLDEN HORDE)

Syr R.

Aral Sea

Amu R.

KHANATE OF PERSIA (IL-KHANS)

Caspian Sea

CAUCASUS MOUNTAINS

Baghdad

Tigris R.

Euphrates R.

Black Sea

Volga R.

Arabian Sea

ARABIA
Medina
Mecca

Aden

N

1,000 miles
1,000 kilometers
500
500
0
0

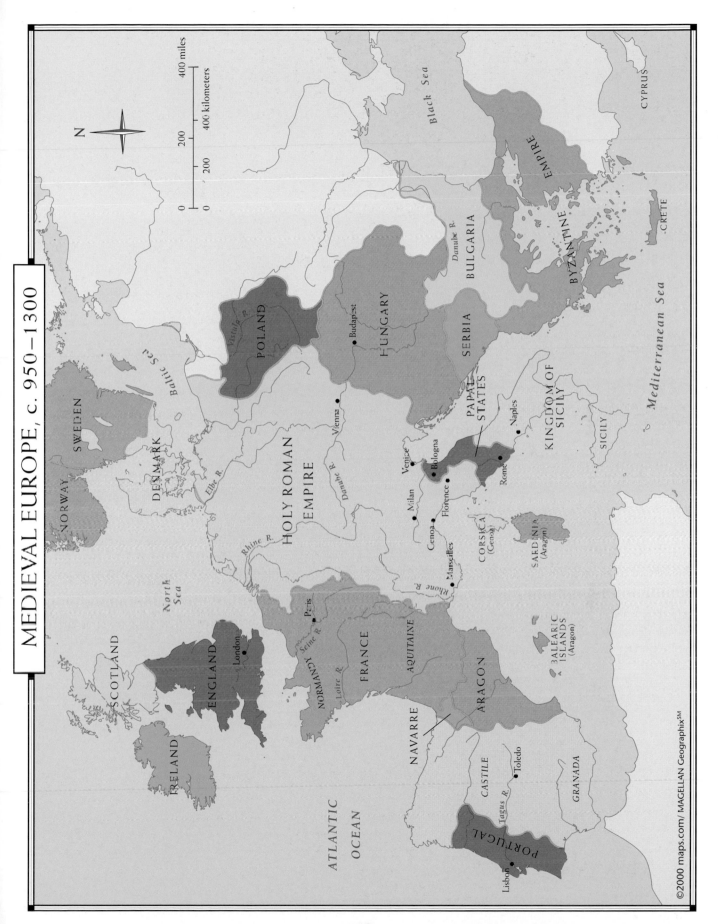

MEDIEVAL EUROPE, c. 950–1300

N

400 miles
400 kilometers
200
200
0
0

ATLANTIC OCEAN

North Sea

Baltic Sea

Black Sea

Mediterranean Sea

SCOTLAND

IRELAND

ENGLAND
London

NORWAY

SWEDEN

DENMARK

Elbe R.

HOLY ROMAN EMPIRE

Rhine R.

Vistula R.

POLAND

Vienna

Danube R.

HUNGARY
Budapest

Danube R.

BULGARIA

SERBIA

BYZANTINE EMPIRE

CYPRUS

CRETE

Seine R.
Paris

NORMANDY

Loire R.

FRANCE

AQUITAINE

Rhone R.

Marseilles

Genoa

Milan

Venice

Florence

Bologna

PAPAL STATES

Rome

Naples

KINGDOM OF SICILY

SICILY

CORSICA (Genoa)

SARDINIA (Aragon)

BALEARIC ISLANDS (Aragon)

NAVARRE

ARAGON

CASTILE

Toledo

Tagus R.

GRANADA

PORTUGAL

Lisbon

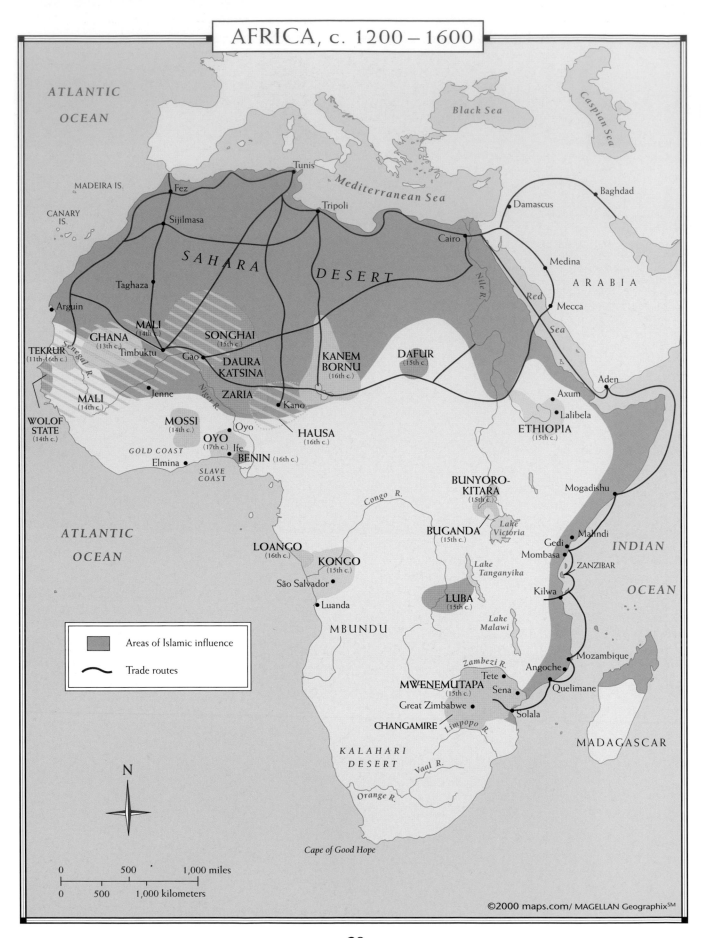

AFRICA, c. 1200–1600

ATLANTIC OCEAN

MADEIRA IS.

CANARY IS.

Black Sea

Caspian Sea

Mediterranean Sea

Tunis

Fez

Sijilmasa

Tripoli

Cairo

Damascus

Baghdad

Medina

Mecca

ARABIA

Red Sea

Nile R.

SAHARA DESERT

Taghaza

Arguin

GHANA
(13th c.)

MALI
(14th c.)

SONGHAI
(15th c.)

Timbuktu

Gao

DAURA
KATSINA

KANEM
BORNU
(16th c.)

DAFUR
(15th c.)

Aden

Axum

Lalibela

TEKRUR
(11th-16th c.)

Senegal R.

Jenne

Niger R.

ZARIA

Kano

ETHIOPIA
(15th c.)

MALI
(14th c.)

WOLOF
STATE
(14th c.)

MOSSI
(14th c.)

Oyo

OYO
(17th c.)

Ife

HAUSA
(16th c.)

GOLD COAST

BENIN (16th c.)

Elmina

SLAVE COAST

BUNYORO-
KITARA
(15th c.)

Mogadishu

Congo R.

BUGANDA
(15th c.)

Lake Victoria

Mahindi

Gedi

INDIAN

ATLANTIC OCEAN

LOANGO
(16th c.)

KONGO
(15th c.)

Lake Tanganyika

Mombasa

ZANZIBAR

São Salvador

LUBA
(15th c.)

Kilwa

OCEAN

Luanda

MBUNDU

Lake Malawi

Mozambique

Zambezi R.

Angoche

Tete

Quelimane

Sena

MWENEMUTAPA
(15th c.)

Great Zimbabwe

Solala

CHANGAMIRE

Limpopo R.

MADAGASCAR

KALAHARI DESERT

Vaal R.

Orange R.

Cape of Good Hope

Legend

▨	Areas of Islamic influence
〜	Trade routes

N

0   500   1,000 miles

0   500   1,000 kilometers

©2000 maps.com/ MAGELLAN Geographix℠

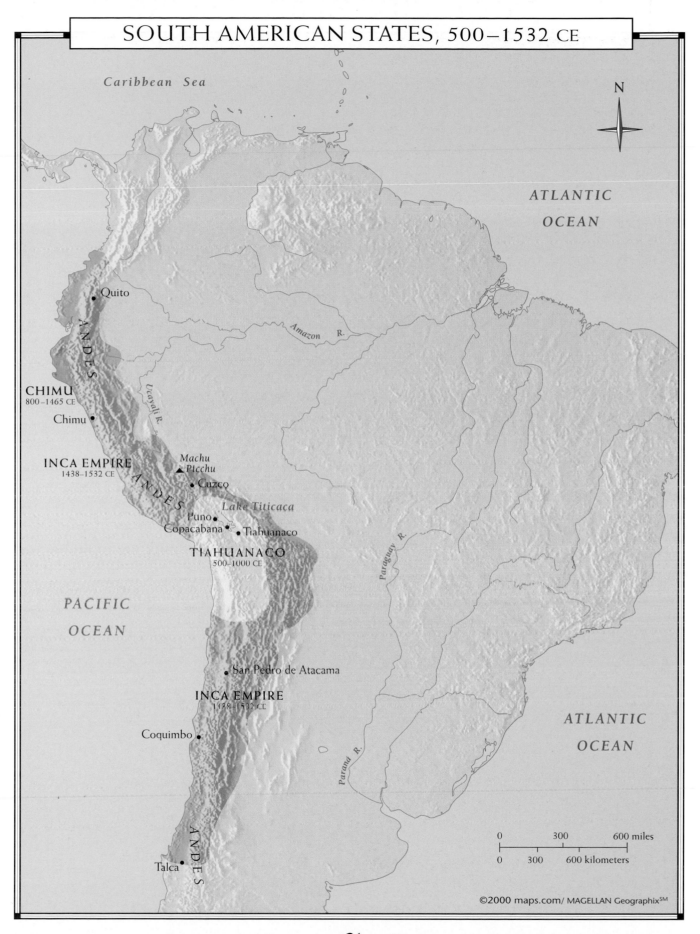

Caribbean Sea

N

ATLANTIC
OCEAN

• Quito

Amazon R.

A
N
D
E
S

CHIMU
800–1465 CE

Chimu •

INCA EMPIRE
1438–1532 CE

A
N
D
E
S

▲ Machu Picchu

• Cuzco

Lake Titicaca

Puno •
Copacabana • • Tiahuanaco

TIAHUANACO
500–1000 CE

Paraguay R.

PACIFIC
OCEAN

Ucayali R.

• San Pedro de Atacama

INCA EMPIRE
1438–1532 CE

ATLANTIC
OCEAN

Coquimbo •

Paraná R.

A
N
D
E
S

Talca •

| 0 | 300 | 600 miles |
| 0 | 300 | 600 kilometers |

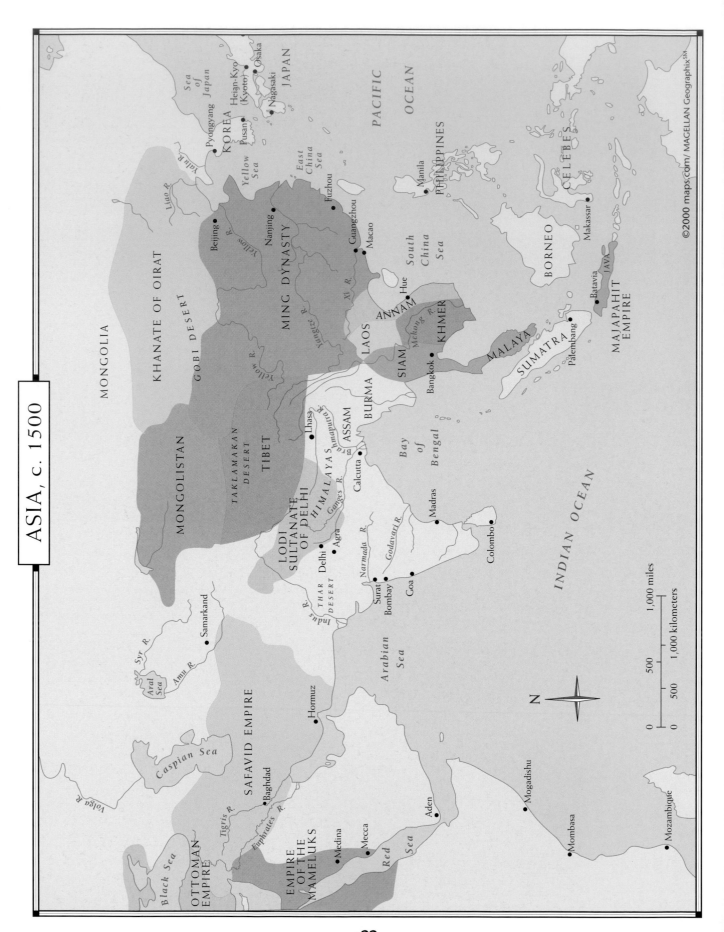

ASIA, c. 1500

MONGOLIA

KHANATE OF OIRAT

GOBI DESERT

MONGOLISTAN

TAKLAMAKAN DESERT

TIBET

MING DYNASTY

KOREA

Pyongyang

Pusan

Heian-Kyo (Kyoto)

Osaka

Nagasaki

JAPAN

Sea of Japan

Yellow Sea

East China Sea

Beijing

Nanjing

Fuzhou

Guangzhou

Macao

PACIFIC OCEAN

PHILIPPINES

Manila

South China Sea

Hue

ANNAM

KHMER

LAOS

SIAM

Bangkok

MALAYA

SUMATRA

Palembang

BORNEO

CELEBES

Makassar

JAVA

Batavia

MAJAPAHIT EMPIRE

BURMA

ASSAM

Lhasa

HIMALAYAS

LODI SULTANATE OF DELHI

Delhi

Agra

THAR DESERT

Ganges R.

Brahmaputra R.

Calcutta

Bay of Bengal

Madras

Narmada R.

Godavari R.

Surat

Bombay

Goa

Colombo

Arabian Sea

Indus R.

Samarkand

Syr R.

Amu R.

Aral Sea

SAFAVID EMPIRE

Hormuz

Caspian Sea

Baghdad

Tigris R.

Euphrates R.

Volga R.

Black Sea

OTTOMAN EMPIRE

EMPIRE OF THE MAMELUKS

Medina

Mecca

Red Sea

Aden

Mogadishu

Mombasa

Mozambique

INDIAN OCEAN

Yalu R.

Liao R.

Yellow R.

Yangtze R.

Yellow R.

Xi R.

Mekong R.

N

0   500   1,000 miles

0   500   1,000 kilometers

©2000 maps.com/ MAGELLAN Geographix℠

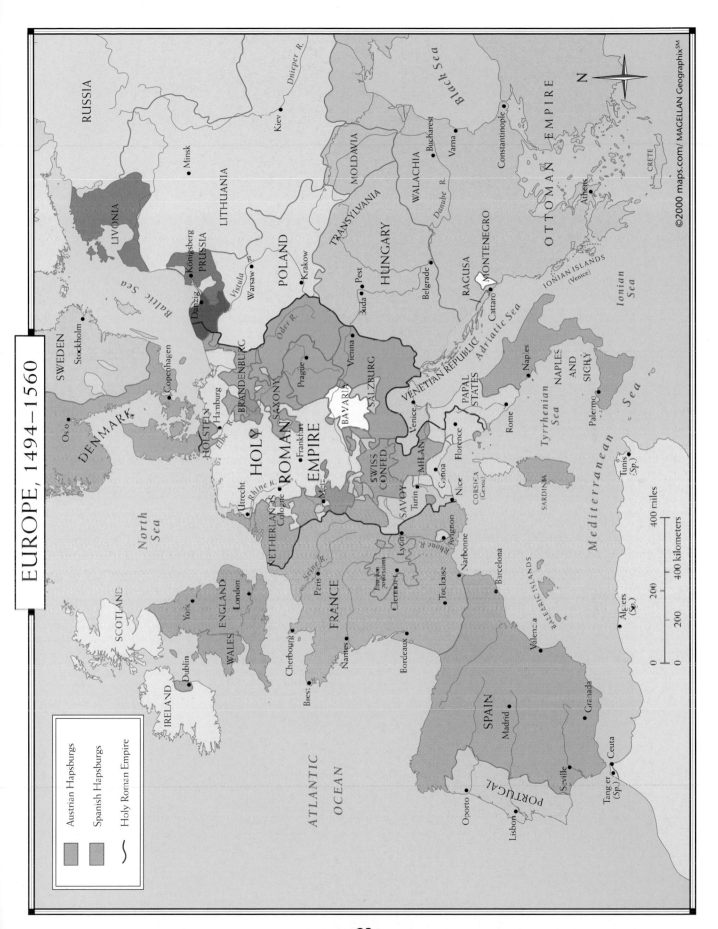

EUROPE, 1494–1560

Legend:
- Austrian Hapsburgs
- Spanish Hapsburgs
- Holy Roman Empire

©2000 maps.com/ MAGELLAN Geographix℠

N

Seas and Oceans:
ATLANTIC OCEAN
North Sea
Baltic Sea
Black Sea
Mediterranean Sea
Adriatic Sea
Ionian Sea
Tyrrhenian Sea

Scale:
0   200   400 miles
0   200   400 kilometers

Regions and Countries:
RUSSIA
SWEDEN
DENMARK
SCOTLAND
IRELAND
WALES
ENGLAND
FRANCE
SPAIN
PORTUGAL
LIVONIA
LITHUANIA
PRUSSIA
POLAND
MOLDAVIA
WALACHIA
TRANSYLVANIA
HUNGARY
HOLY ROMAN EMPIRE
HOLSTEIN
BRANDENBURG
SAXONY
BAVARIA
SALZBURG
SWISS CONFED.
SAVOY
MILAN
NETHERLANDS
VENETIAN REPUBLIC
PAPAL STATES
NAPLES
NAPLES AND SICILY
MONTENEGRO
RAGUSA
OTTOMAN EMPIRE
IONIAN ISLANDS (Venice)
CRETE
CORSICA (Genoa)
SARDINIA
BALEARIC ISLANDS
Foreign possessions

Cities:
Kiev
Minsk
Königsberg
Danzig
Warsaw
Krakow
Stockholm
Copenhagen
Oslo
Hamburg
Prague
Vienna
Buda
Pest
Belgrade
Bucharest
Varna
Constantinople
Athens
Cattaro
Venice
Rome
Florence
Genoa
Nice
Milan
Turin
Naples
Palermo
Tunis (Sp.)
Algiers (Sp.)
Valencia
Barcelona
Madrid
Granada
Seville
Lisbon
Oporto
Ceuta
Tanger (Sp.)
Narbonne
Toulouse
Avignon
Lyon
Clermont
Bordeaux
Nantes
Brest
Cherbourg
Paris
Metz
Cologne
Utrecht
Frankfurt
London
York
Dublin

Rivers:
Dnieper R.
Vistula R.
Oder R.
Elbe R.
Rhine R.
Seine R.
Rhone R.
Danube R.

-23-

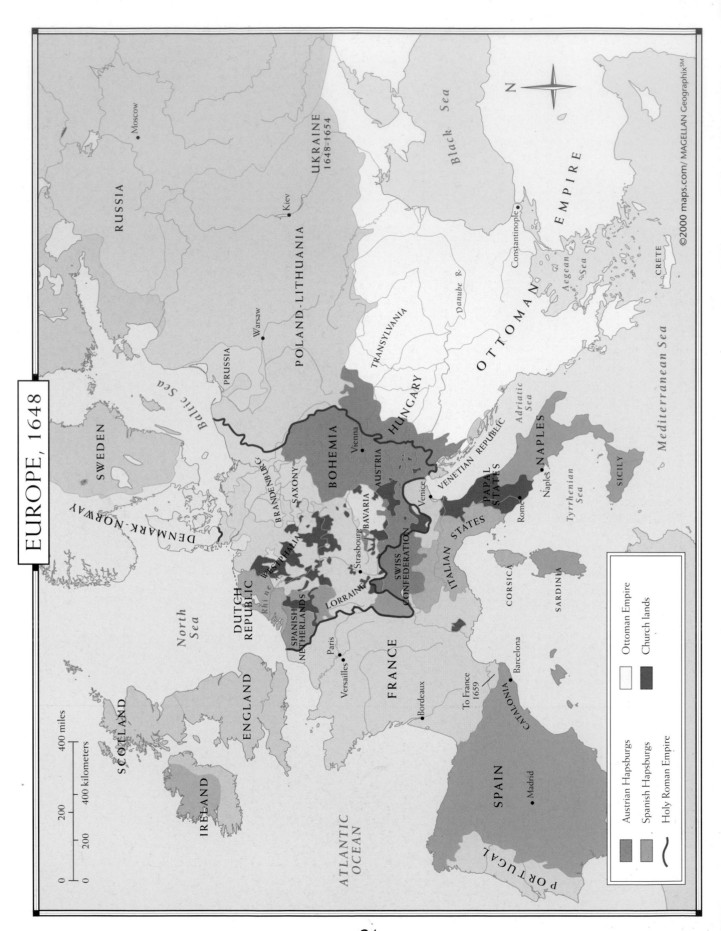

EUROPE, 1648

©2000 maps.com/ MAGELLAN Geographix℠

SWEDEN

DENMARK-NORWAY

RUSSIA

Moscow

Kiev

UKRAINE
1648-1654

POLAND-LITHUANIA

Warsaw

PRUSSIA

Baltic Sea

BRANDENBURG

SAXONY

BOHEMIA

Vienna

AUSTRIA

HUNGARY

TRANSYLVANIA

Danube R.

OTTOMAN EMPIRE

Black Sea

Constantinople

Aegean Sea

CRETE

BAVARIA

WESTPHALIA

Strasbourg

Rhine

SWISS
CONFEDERATION

ITALIAN STATES

VENETIAN REPUBLIC

Venice

Adriatic Sea

PAPAL STATES

Rome

NAPLES

Naples

Tyrrhenian Sea

SICILY

Mediterranean Sea

SCOTLAND

ENGLAND

IRELAND

North Sea

DUTCH REPUBLIC

SPANISH
NETHERLANDS

LORRAINE

Paris

Versailles

FRANCE

Bordeaux

To France
1659

Barcelona

CATALONIA

CORSICA

SARDINIA

ATLANTIC OCEAN

SPAIN

Madrid

PORTUGAL

400 miles

400 kilometers

200

200

0

0

Austrian Hapsburgs

Spanish Hapsburgs

Holy Roman Empire

Ottoman Empire

Church lands

N

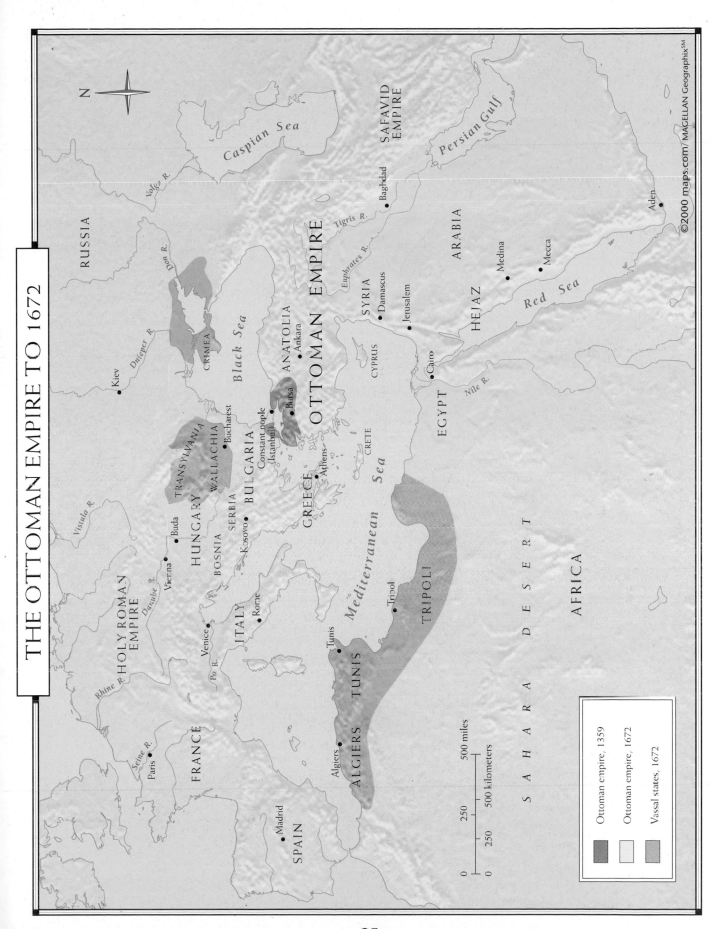

THE OTTOMAN EMPIRE TO 1672

N

RUSSIA

Caspian Sea

SAFAVID EMPIRE

Persian Gulf

Volga R.

Baghdad

Tigris R.

Aden

Don R.

ARABIA

Kiev

Dnieper R.

CRIMEA

Black Sea

OTTOMAN EMPIRE

Euphrates R.

HEJAZ

Medina

Mecca

Red Sea

SYRIA

Damascus

ANATOLIA

Ankara

Jerusalem

Bursa

CYPRUS

Cairo

Nile R.

EGYPT

Constant-nople
(Istanbul)

TRANSYLVANIA

Bucharest

WALLACHIA

BULGARIA

GREECE

Athens

CRETE

Mediterranean Sea

Vistula R.

Buda

SERBIA

HUNGARY

BOSNIA

Kosovo

Vienna

Danube

Rome

ITALY

Po R.

Venice

TRIPOLI

Tripoli

SAHARA DESERT

AFRICA

Rhine R.

HOLY ROMAN EMPIRE

Mediterranean

Tunis

TUNIS

FRANCE

Seine R.

Paris

ALGIERS

Algiers

Madrid

SPAIN

500 miles

500 kilometers

250

500

250

250

0

0

	Ottoman empire, 1359
	Ottoman empire, 1672
	Vassal states, 1672

©2000 maps.com/ MAGELLAN Geographix℠

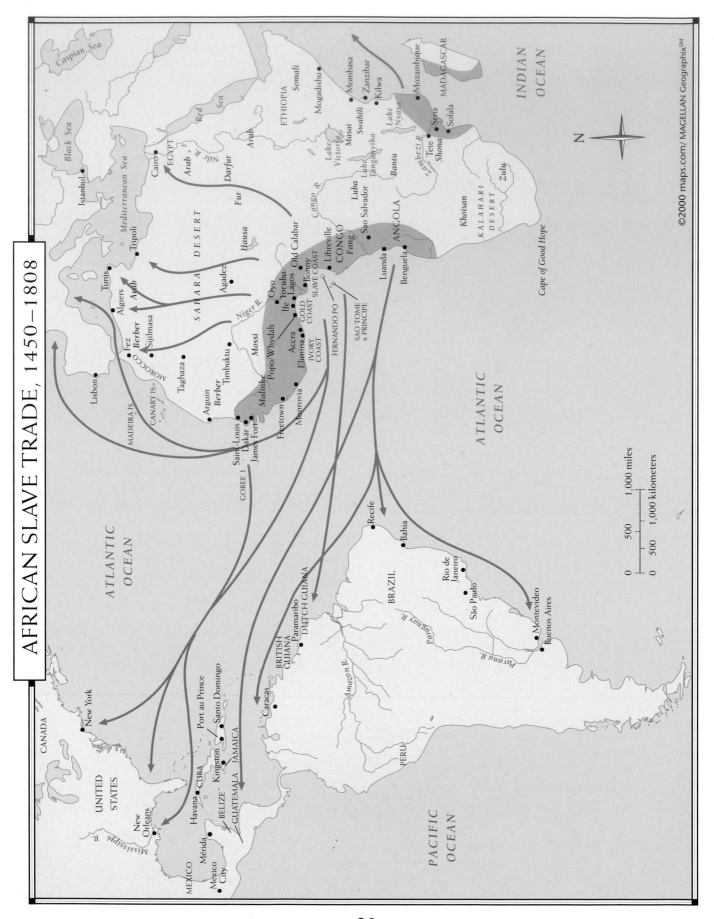

AFRICAN SLAVE TRADE, 1450–1808

©2000 maps.com/ MAGELLAN Geographix℠

INDIAN OCEAN

N

ATLANTIC OCEAN

PACIFIC OCEAN

Caspian Sea

Black Sea

Istanbul

Mediterranean Sea

Red Sea

Tripoli

Tunis

Algiers

Fez

Sijilmasa

MOROCCO

Berber

Berber

Arab

Arab

SAHARA DESERT

Cairo

EGYPT

Nile R.

Arab

Darfur

Fur

ETHIOPIA

Somali

Mogadishu

Mombasa

Zanzibar

Kilwa

Mozambique

MADAGASCAR

Sena

Sofala

Tete

Shona

Zambezi R.

Lake Nyasa

Swahili

Masai

Bantu

Zulu

Lake Victoria

Lake Tanganyika

Luba

Khoisan

KALAHARI DESERT

Cape of Good Hope

Congo R.

Sao Salvador

CONGO

Fang

ANGOLA

Luanda

Benguela

Libreville

Old Calabar

Bonny

SLAVE COAST

FERNANDO PO

SAO TOME & PRINCIPE

Lagos

Yoruba

Oyo

Ife

Accra

Elmina

GOLD COAST

IVORY COAST

Popo/Whydah

Mossi

Malinke

Hausa

Agadez

Niger R.

Timbuktu

Taghaza

Arguin

Berber

Saint-Louis

Dakar

James Fort

GOREE I.

Freetown

Monrovia

CANARY IS.

MADERA IS.

Lisbon

Montevideo

Buenos Aires

São Paulo

Rio de Janeiro

BRAZIL

Bahia

Recife

Paramaribo

DUTCH GUIANA

BRITISH GUIANA

Amazon R.

Paraguay R.

Parana R.

PERU

Caracas

Port au Prince

Santo Domingo

Kingston

JAMAICA

CUBA

Havana

BELIZE

GUATEMALA

Mérida

MEXICO

Mexico City

New Orleans

Mississippi R.

UNITED STATES

CANADA

New York

ATLANTIC OCEAN

0   500   1,000 miles

0   500   1,000 kilometers

EXPLORATION AND COLONIZATION, c. 1700

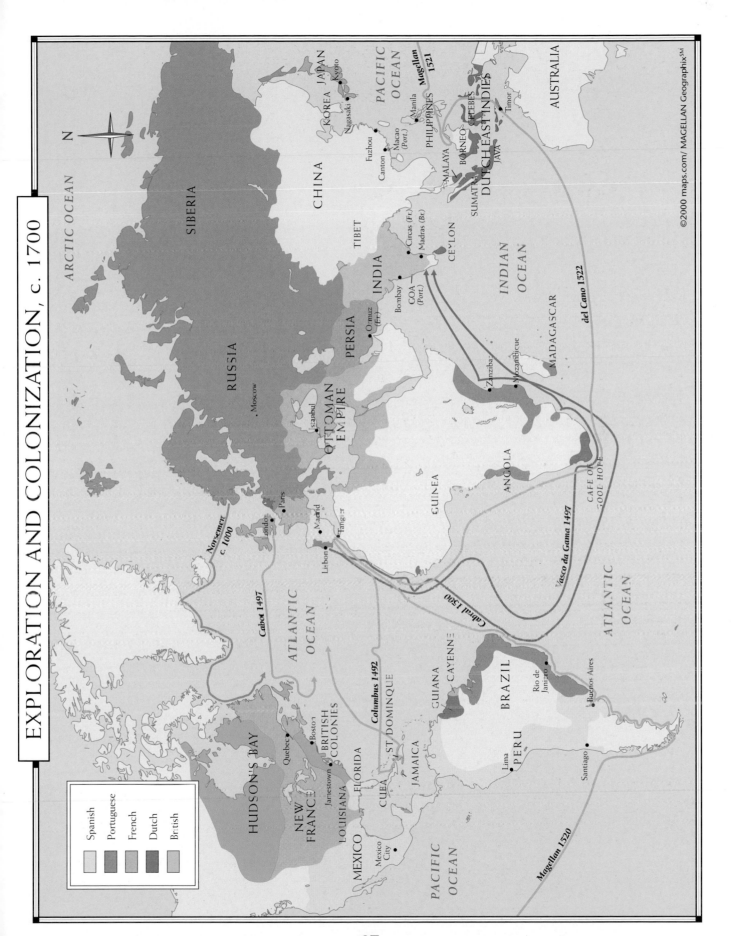

Legend:
- Spanish
- Portuguese
- French
- Dutch
- British

ARCTIC OCEAN

SIBERIA

JAPAN
Kyoto
KOREA
Nagasaki
CHINA
Fuzhou
Canton
Macao (Port.)
Manila
PHILIPPINES
BORNEO
CELEBES
SUMATRA
MALAYA
JAVA
DUTCH EAST INDIES
Timor
AUSTRALIA

PACIFIC OCEAN

Magellan 1521

©2000 maps.com/ MAGELLAN Geographix℠

TIBET
INDIA
Circas (Fr.)
Madras (Br.)
CEYLON
Bombay
GOA (Port.)
O-muz (Fr.)
PERSIA
OTTOMAN EMPIRE
Istanbul
RUSSIA
Moscow

INDIAN OCEAN
MADAGASCAR
Zanzibar
Mozambique
ANGOLA
GUINEA
CAPE OF GOOD HOPE

del Camo 1522
Vasco da Gama 1497
Cabral 1500

Paris
London
Madrid
Tangier
Lisbon

Norsemen c. 1000
Cabot 1497

ATLANTIC OCEAN

Columbus 1492

HUDSON'S BAY
Quebec
Boston
BRITISH COLONIES
Jamestown
NEW FRANCE
FLORIDA
LOUISIANA
ST. DOMINGUE
JAMAICA
CUBA
MEXICO
Mexico City

GUIANA
CAYENNE
GUIANA
BRAZIL
Rio de Janiaro
Buenos Aires
PERU
Lima
Santiago

ATLANTIC OCEAN

Magellan 1520

PACIFIC OCEAN

N

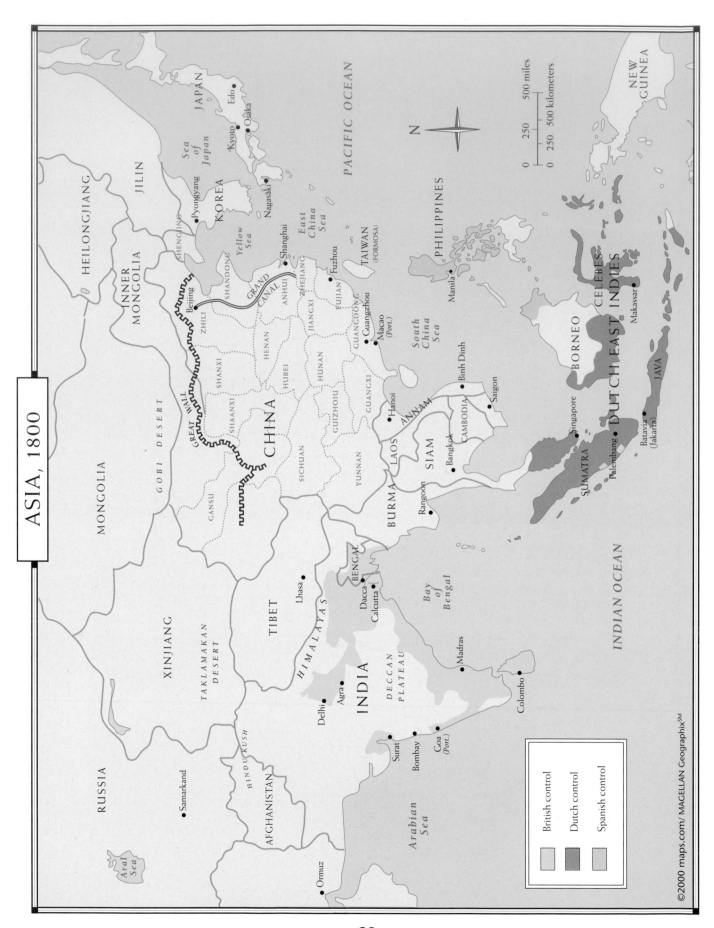

ASIA, 1800

RUSSIA

MONGOLIA

HEILONGJIANG

JILIN

INNER MONGOLIA

SHENGJING

Sea of Japan

Pyongyang

KOREA

JAPAN

Edo

Kyoto

Osaka

Nagasaki

Yellow Sea

Beijing

ZHILI

SHANDONG

GRAND CANAL

Shanghai

East China Sea

ANHUI

ZHEJIANG

JIANGXI

FUJIAN

Fuzhou

TAIWAN (FORMOSA)

PACIFIC OCEAN

N

500 miles

250

500 kilometers

250

0

0

NEW GUINEA

PHILIPPINES

Manila

GREAT WALL

GOBI DESERT

SHANXI

HENAN

SHAANXI

HUBEI

HUNAN

CHINA

GANSU

SICHUAN

GUIZHOIU

GUANGXI

YUNNAN

GUANGDONG

Guangzhou

Macao (Port.)

South China Sea

Hanoi

ANNAM

Binh Dinh

Saigon

BORNEO

CELEBES

Makassar

DUTCH EAST INDIES

JAVA

XINJIANG

TAKLAMAKAN DESERT

TIBET

Lhasa

HINDU KUSH

AFGHANISTAN

HIMALAYAS

LAOS

BURMA

Rangoon

SIAM

Bangkok

CAMBODIA

Singapore

SUMATRA

Palembang

Batavia (Jakarta)

Samarkand

Delhi

Agra

INDIA

DECCAN PLATEAU

BENGAL

Dacca

Calcutta

Bay of Bengal

Madras

Colombo

Surat

Bombay

Goa (Port.)

Arabian Sea

Ormuz

Aral Sea

INDIAN OCEAN

British control

Dutch control

Spanish control

©2000 maps.com/ MAGELLAN Geographix℠

—28—

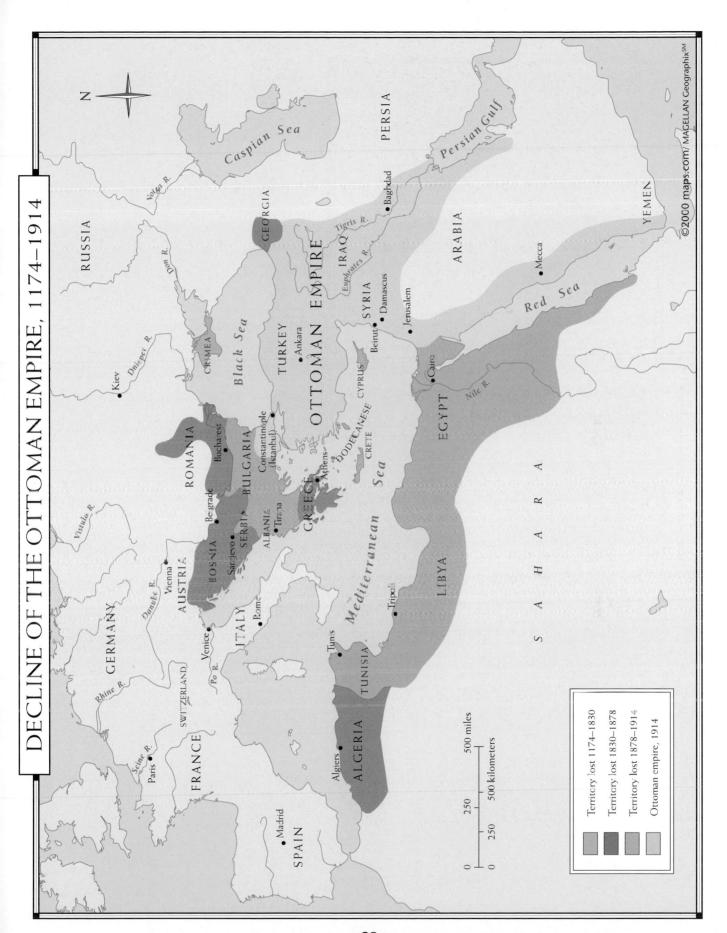

DECLINE OF THE OTTOMAN EMPIRE, 1174–1914

©2000 maps.com/ MAGELLAN Geographix℠

N

RUSSIA

Caspian Sea

GEORGIA

PERSIA

Persian Gulf

Volta R.

Tigris R.

Baghdad

Dnieper R.

Don R.

Kiev

CRIMEA

Black Sea

TURKEY

Ankara

OTTOMAN EMPIRE

IRAQ

Euphrates R.

SYRIA

Damascus

Beirut

ARABIA

YEMEN

Mecca

Jerusalem

Red Sea

Vistula R.

GERMANY

AUSTRIA

Danube R.

Vienna

ROMANIA

Bucharest

BULGARIA

Constantinople
(Istanbul)

Athens

GREECE

Belgrade

BOSNIA

Sarajevo

SERBIA

ALBANIA

Tirana

DODECANESE

CYPRUS

Cairo

Nile R.

EGYPT

CRETE

SWITZERLAND

Rhine R.

FRANCE

Po R.

Seine R.

Paris

ITALY

Venice

Rome

Mediterranean Sea

Tripoli

LIBYA

S A H A R A

Tunis

TUNISIA

Madrid

SPAIN

Algiers

ALGERIA

500 miles

500 kilometers

250   500

0   0

	Territory lost 1174–1830
	Territory lost 1830–1878
	Territory lost 1878–1914
	Ottoman empire, 1914

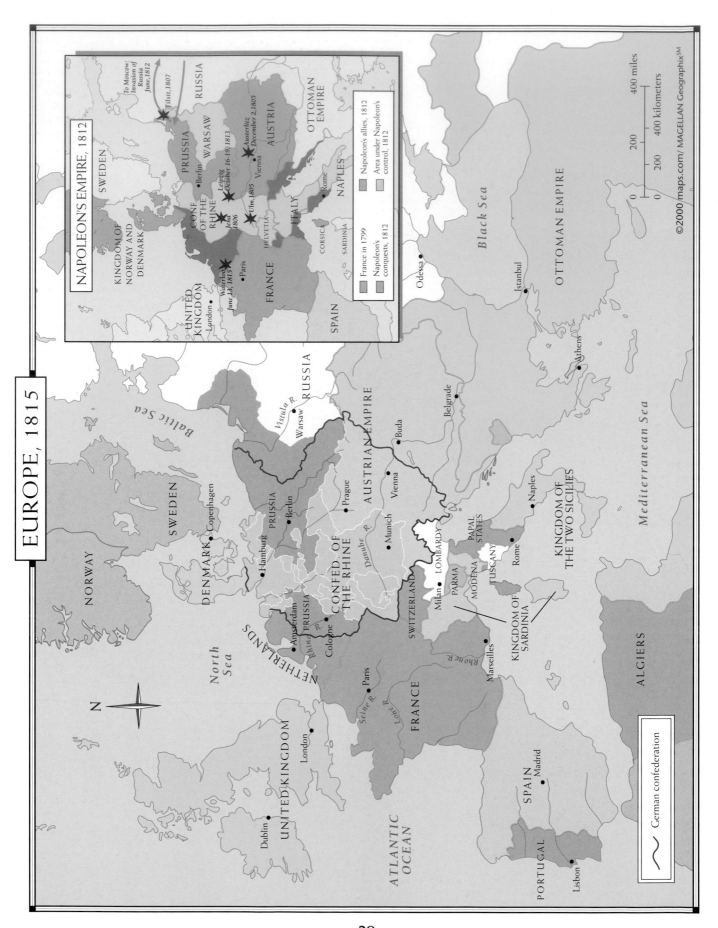

EUROPE, 1815

NAPOLEON'S EMPIRE, 1812

To Moscow: Invasion of Russia June, 1812

SWEDEN

RUSSIA

PRUSSIA

WARSAW

Tilsit, 1807

Berlin

Leipzig October 16–19, 1813

KINGDOM OF NORWAY AND DENMARK

CONF. OF THE RHINE

Jena 1806

Austerlitz December 2, 1805

Vienna

AUSTRIA

Ulm, 1805

OTTOMAN EMPIRE

UNITED KINGDOM

London

Waterloo June 18, 1815

Paris

FRANCE

HELVETIA

ITALY

Rome

CORSICA

SARDINIA

NAPLES

SPAIN

France in 1799	Napoleon's allies, 1812
Napoleon's conquests, 1812	Area under Napoleon's control, 1812

ATLANTIC OCEAN

NORWAY

SWEDEN

North Sea

Baltic Sea

DENMARK

Copenhagen

Hamburg

PRUSSIA

Berlin

Vistula R.

Warsaw

RUSSIA

UNITED KINGDOM

Dublin

London

NETHERLANDS

Amsterdam

Rhine R.

Cologne

CONFED. OF THE RHINE

Prague

Danube R.

Munich

Vienna

AUSTRIAN EMPIRE

Buda

Belgrade

Odessa

Black Sea

SWITZERLAND

Seine R.

Paris

Loire R.

FRANCE

Marseilles

Rhône R.

LOMBARDY

Milan

PARMA

MODENA

TUSCANY

KINGDOM OF SARDINIA

PAPAL STATES

Rome

Naples

KINGDOM OF THE TWO SICILIES

Athens

OTTOMAN EMPIRE

Istanbul

Mediterranean Sea

ALGIERS

SPAIN

Madrid

PORTUGAL

Lisbon

N

⌒	German confederation

©2000 maps.com / MAGELLAN Geographix℠

0   200   400 miles

0   200   400 kilometers

—30—

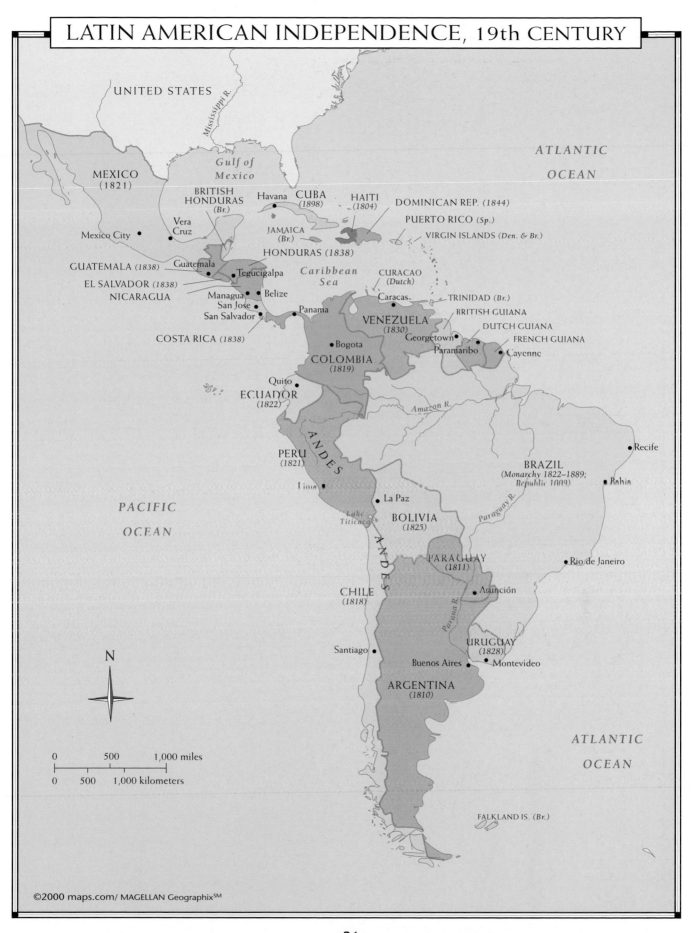

UNITED STATES

Mississippi R.

ATLANTIC OCEAN

Gulf of Mexico

MEXICO (1821)

BRITISH HONDURAS (Br.)

Havana

CUBA (1898)

HAITI (1804)

DOMINICAN REP. (1844)

PUERTO RICO (Sp.)

VIRGIN ISLANDS (Den. & Br.)

Vera Cruz

JAMAICA (Br.)

Mexico City

HONDURAS (1838)

GUATEMALA (1838)   Guatemala

EL SALVADOR (1838)   Tegucigalpa

NICARAGUA   Managua   Belize

San Jose

San Salvador

COSTA RICA (1838)

Panama

Caribbean Sea

CURACAO (Dutch)

Caracas

TRINIDAD (Br.)

BRITISH GUIANA

DUTCH GUIANA

FRENCH GUIANA

Georgetown

Paramaribo

Cayenne

VENEZUELA (1830)

Bogota

COLOMBIA (1819)

Quito

ECUADOR (1822)

Amazon R.

PERU (1821)

ANDES

Lima

La Paz

Recife

BRAZIL (Monarchy 1822–1889; Republic 1889)

Bahia

Lake Titicaca

BOLIVIA (1825)

Paraguay R.

PACIFIC OCEAN

ANDES

PARAGUAY (1811)

Rio de Janeiro

CHILE (1818)

Asunción

Parana R.

Santiago

URUGUAY (1828)

Buenos Aires   Montevideo

ARGENTINA (1810)

ATLANTIC OCEAN

N

0   500   1,000 miles

0   500   1,000 kilometers

FALKLAND IS. (Br.)

INDUSTRIALIZATION AND URBANIZATION IN EUROPE, c. 1850

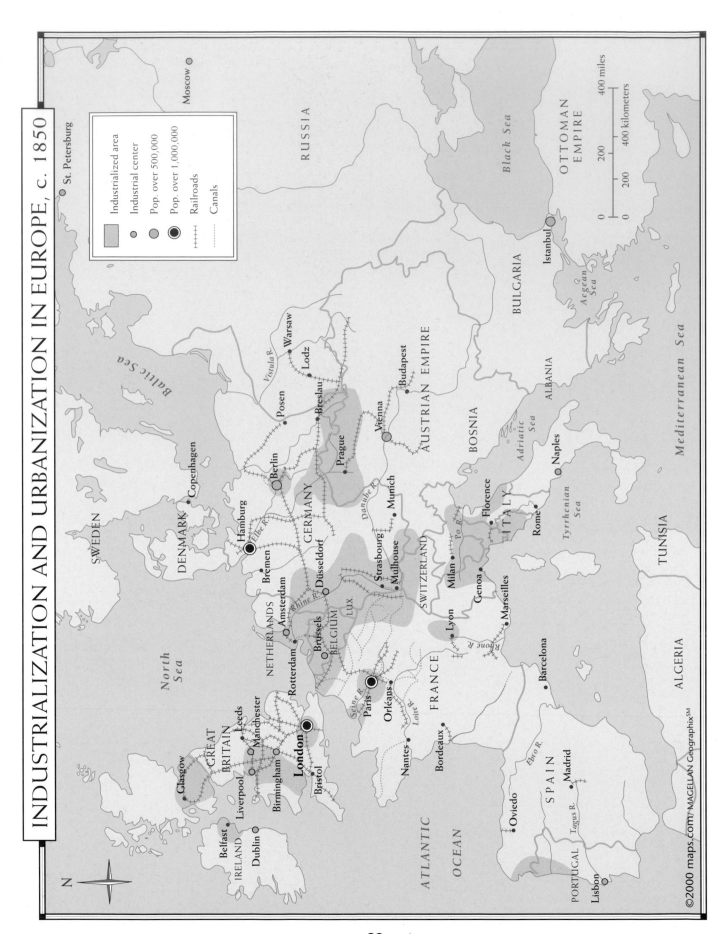

Legend
- Industrialized area
- Industrial center
- Pop. over 500,000
- Pop. over 1,000,000
- Railroads
- Canals

N

St. Petersburg

Moscow

RUSSIA

SWEDEN

Baltic Sea

Copenhagen

DENMARK

Warsaw

Lodz

Posen

Breslau

Prague

Vistula R.

Berlin

Hamburg

Elbe R.

GERMANY

Bremen

Amsterdam

Rhine R.

NETHERLANDS

Rotterdam

Brussels

BELGIUM

LUX.

Düsseldorf

Strasbourg

Mulhouse

Munich

Danube R.

Vienna

Budapest

AUSTRIAN EMPIRE

SWITZERLAND

Milan

Genoa

Po R.

Florence

ITALY

Rome

Naples

BOSNIA

BULGARIA

ALBANIA

Adriatic Sea

Tyrrhenian Sea

Aegean Sea

Black Sea

OTTOMAN EMPIRE

Istanbul

Mediterranean Sea

TUNISIA

ALGERIA

North Sea

GREAT BRITAIN

Glasgow

Leeds

Manchester

Liverpool

Birmingham

Bristol

London

IRELAND

Belfast

Dublin

ATLANTIC OCEAN

Lyon

Marseilles

Rhone R.

Seine R.

Paris

Orléans

Loire R.

FRANCE

Nantes

Bordeaux

Barcelona

Madrid

SPAIN

Ebro R.

Oviedo

Tagus R.

PORTUGAL

Lisbon

400 miles

400 kilometers

200

200

0

0

IMPERIALISM IN THE MODERN WORLD, 1900

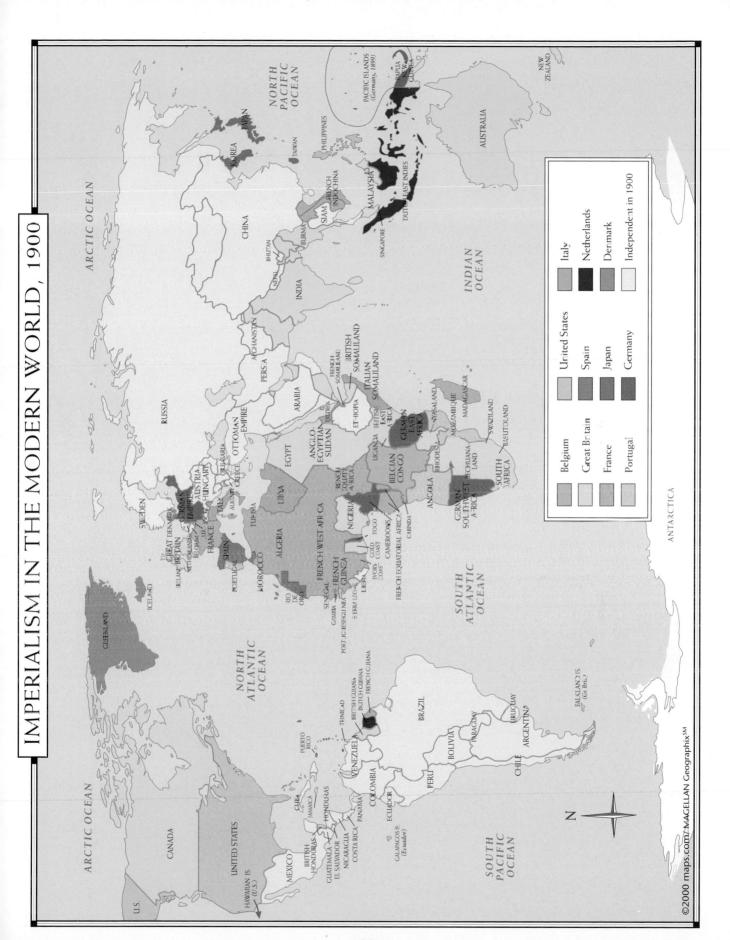

Legend:

Belgium	United States	Italy
Great Britain	Spain	Netherlands
France	Japan	Denmark
Portugal	Germany	Independent in 1900

ASIAN IMPERIALISM TO 1910

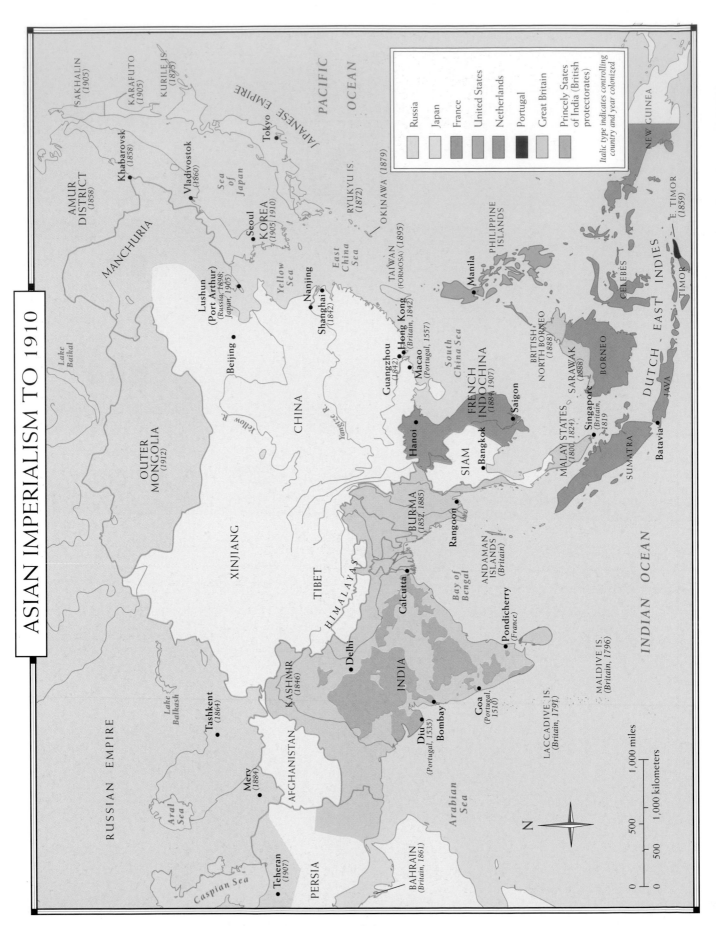

Legend:
- Russia
- Japan
- France
- United States
- Netherlands
- Portugal
- Great Britain
- Princely States of India (British protectorates)

Italic type indicates controlling country and year colonized

SAKHALIN (1905)
KARAFUTO (1905)
KURILE IS. (1875)
JAPANESE EMPIRE
PACIFIC OCEAN
AMUR DISTRICT (1858)
Khabarovsk (1858)
Vladivostok (1860)
Sea of Japan
Tokyo
MANCHURIA
Seoul
KOREA (1905, 1910)
East China Sea
RYUKYU IS. (1872)
OKINAWA (1879)
Lushun (Port Arthur) (Russia, 1898; Japan, 1905)
Nanjing
Yellow Sea
TAIWAN (FORMOSA) (1895)
Beijing
Shanghai (1842)
Hong Kong (Britain, 1842)
Guangzhou (1842)
Macao (Portugal, 1557)
South China Sea
PHILIPPINE ISLANDS
Manila
NEW GUINEA
E. TIMOR (1859)
TIMOR
CELEBES
DUTCH EAST INDIES
BRITISH NORTH BORNEO (1888)
SARAWAK (1888)
BORNEO
FRENCH INDOCHINA (1884, 1907)
Hanoi
Saigon
MALAY STATES (1800, 1824)
Singapore (Britain, 1819)
SUMATRA
JAVA
Batavia
Lake Baikal
OUTER MONGOLIA (1912)
CHINA
Yellow R.
Yangtze R.
XINJIANG
TIBET
HIMALAYAS
SIAM
Bangkok
BURMA (1852, 1885)
Rangoon
ANDAMAN ISLANDS (Britain)
Bay of Bengal
RUSSIAN EMPIRE
Lake Balkash
Tashkent (1864)
KASHMIR (1846)
INDIA
Delhi
Calcutta
Pondicherry (France)
Aral Sea
AFGHANISTAN
Merv (1884)
Goa (Portugal, 1510)
Diu (Portugal, 1535)
Bombay
MALDIVE IS. (Britain, 1796)
LACCADIVE IS. (Britain, 1791)
INDIAN OCEAN
Arabian Sea
BAHRAIN (Britain, 1861)
PERSIA
Teheran (1907)
Caspian Sea

N

1,000 miles
1,000 kilometers
500
500
0
0

—34—

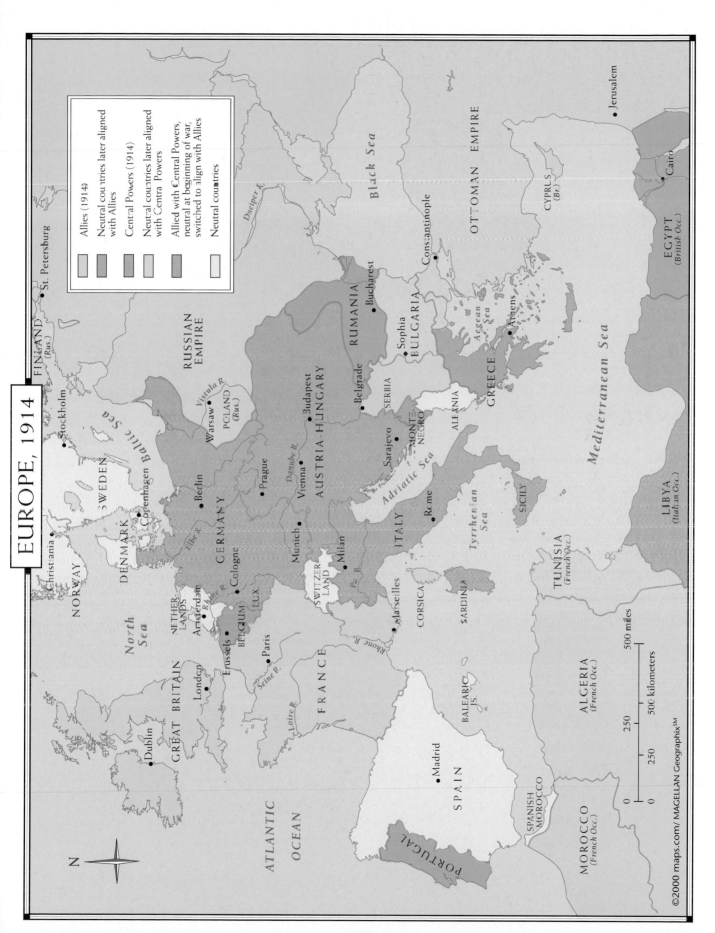

EUROPE, 1914

Legend:
- Allies (1914)
- Neutral countries later aligned with Allies
- Central Powers (1914)
- Neutral countries later aligned with Central Powers
- Allied with Central Powers, neutral at beginning of war, switched to align with Allies
- Neutral countries

N

ATLANTIC OCEAN

GREAT BRITAIN
- Dublin
- London

NORWAY
- Christiania

SWEDEN
- Stockholm

FINLAND (Rus.)
- St. Petersburg

North Sea

Baltic Sea

DENMARK
- Copenhagen

NETHERLANDS
- Amsterdam

BELGIUM
- Brussels

LUX.

FRANCE
- Paris
- Marseilles

Seine R.
Loire R.
Rhône R.

GERMANY
- Berlin
- Cologne
- Munich

Elbe R.
Rhine R.

RUSSIAN EMPIRE

Dnieper R.

POLAND (Rus.)
- Warsaw

Vistula R.

SWITZERLAND

Po R.

ITALY
- Rome
- Milan

AUSTRIA-HUNGARY
- Vienna
- Prague
- Budapest

Danube R.

RUMANIA
- Bucharest

SERBIA
- Belgrade
- Sarajevo

MONTENEGRO

ALBANIA

BULGARIA
- Sophia

GREECE
- Athens

Black Sea

Adriatic Sea

Tyrrhenian Sea

CORSICA

SARDINIA

SICILY

Aegean Sea

OTTOMAN EMPIRE
- Constantinople

CYPRUS (Br.)

Mediterranean Sea

SPAIN
- Madrid

PORTUGAL

BALEARIC IS.

SPANISH MOROCCO

MOROCCO (French Occ.)

ALGERIA (French Occ.)

TUNISIA (French Occ.)

LIBYA (Italian Occ.)

EGYPT (British Occ.)
- Cairo

- Jerusalem

Scale:
500 miles
250
0

500 kilometers
250
0

©2000 maps.com/ MAGELLAN Geographix℠

-35-

AFRICA, 1914

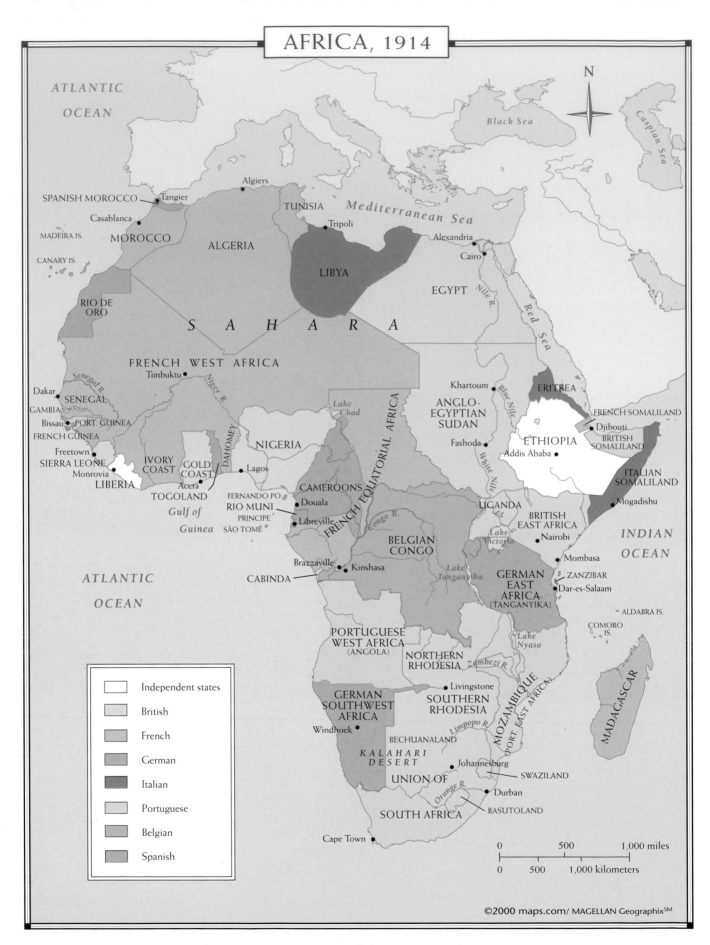

ATLANTIC OCEAN

N

Black Sea

Caspian Sea

SPANISH MOROCCO — Tangier
Algiers
Casablanca
MADEIRA IS.
MOROCCO
TUNISIA
Mediterranean Sea
Tripoli
Alexandria
Cairo
CANARY IS.
ALGERIA
LIBYA
EGYPT
Nile R.
RIO DE ORO
SAHARA
Red Sea
FRENCH WEST AFRICA
Timbuktu
Senegal R.
Dakar
SENEGAL
Niger R.
GAMBIA
Bissau
PORT. GUINEA
FRENCH GUINEA
DAHOMEY
NIGERIA
Lake Chad
Khartoum
ANGLO-EGYPTIAN SUDAN
Blue Nile
ERITREA
FRENCH SOMALILAND
Djibouti
BRITISH SOMALILAND
Freetown
SIERRA LEONE
IVORY COAST
GOLD COAST
Lagos
Fashoda
White Nile
ETHIOPIA
Addis Ababa
Monrovia
Accra
LIBERIA
TOGOLAND
Gulf of Guinea
CAMEROONS
FERNANDO PO
RIO MUNI
Douala
FRENCH EQUATORIAL AFRICA
UGANDA
BRITISH EAST AFRICA
ITALIAN SOMALILAND
Mogadishu
PRINCIPE
SÃO TOMÉ
Libreville
Congo R.
Lake Victoria
Nairobi
INDIAN OCEAN
BELGIAN CONGO
Mombasa
Brazzaville
Kinshasa
ZANZIBAR
CABINDA
Lake Tanganyika
GERMAN EAST AFRICA (TANGANYIKA)
Dar-es-Salaam
ATLANTIC OCEAN
ALDABRA IS.
COMORO IS.
PORTUGUESE WEST AFRICA (ANGOLA)
NORTHERN RHODESIA
Lake Nyasa
Zambezi R.
MADAGASCAR
GERMAN SOUTHWEST AFRICA
Livingstone
SOUTHERN RHODESIA
MOZAMBIQUE (PORT. EAST AFRICA)
Windhoek
BECHUANALAND
KALAHARI DESERT
Limpopo R.
Johannesburg
SWAZILAND
UNION OF SOUTH AFRICA
Orange R.
Durban
BASUTOLAND
Cape Town

Legend:
- Independent states
- British
- French
- German
- Italian
- Portuguese
- Belgian
- Spanish

0   500   1,000 miles
0   500   1,000 kilometers

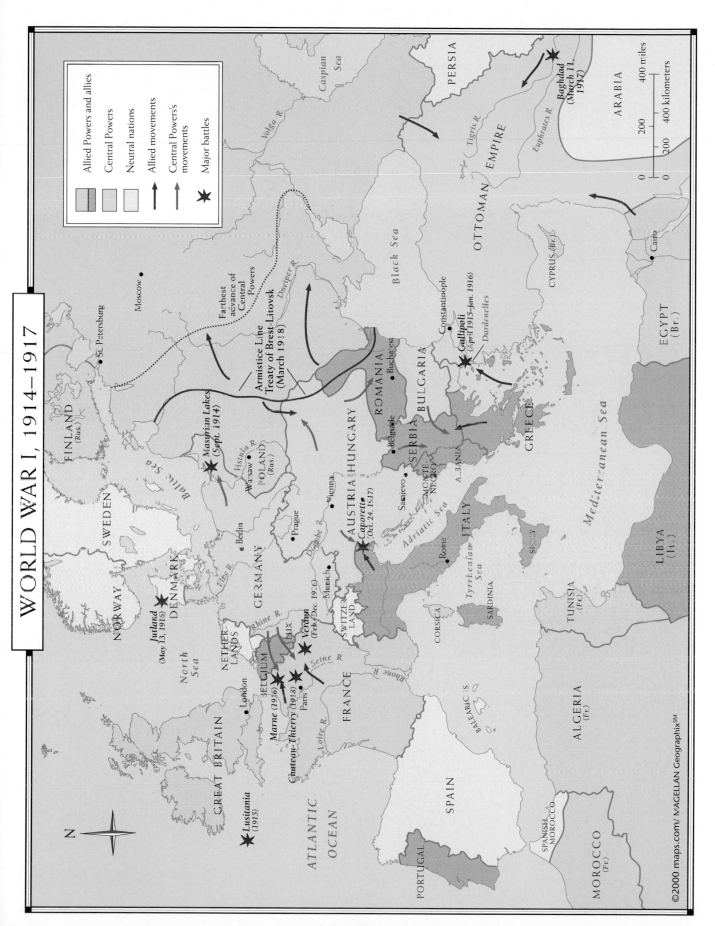

WORLD WAR I, 1914–1917

Allied Powers and allies
Central Powers
Neutral nations
Allied movements
Central Powers's movements
Major battles

N

St. Petersburg
Moscow
FINLAND (Rus.)
SWEDEN
NORWAY
Baltic Sea
North Sea
GREAT BRITAIN
London
ATLANTIC OCEAN
Lusitania (1915)
Jutland (May 13, 1915)
DENMARK
NETHER-LANDS
BELGIUM
LUX.
Berlin
GERMANY
Elbe R.
Rhine R.
Prague
Munich
SWITZER-LAND
Verdun (Feb.–Dec. 1916)
Marne (1916)
Chateau-Thierry (1918)
Paris
Seine R.
Loire R.
Rhone R.
FRANCE
SPAIN
PORTUGAL
MOROCCO (Fr.)
SPANISH MOROCCO
ALGERIA (Fr.)
BALEARIC IS.
CORSICA
SARDINIA
TUNISIA (Fr.)
ITALY
Rome
Tyrrhenian Sea
SICILY
LIBYA (It.)
Mediterranean Sea
Adriatic Sea
AUSTRIA-HUNGARY
Vienna
Danube R.
Caporetto (Oct. 24, 1917)
A. BANIA
MONTE-NEGRO
Sarajevo
SERBIA
Belgrade
BULGARIA
ROMANIA
Bucharest
Masurian Lakes (Sept. 1914)
Warsaw
Vistula R.
POLAND (Rus.)
Armistice Line Treaty of Brest-Litovsk (March 1918)
Farthest advance of Central Powers
Dnieper R.
Volga R.
Black Sea
Caspian Sea
Constantinople
Gallipoli (April 1915–Jan. 1916)
Dardanelles
GREECE
OTTOMAN EMPIRE
PERSIA
Tigris R.
Euphrates R.
Baghdad (March 11, 1917)
ARABIA
CYPRUS (Br.)
Cairo
EGYPT (Br.)

0   200   400 miles
0   200   400 kilometers

©2000 maps.com/MAGELLAN Geographix℠

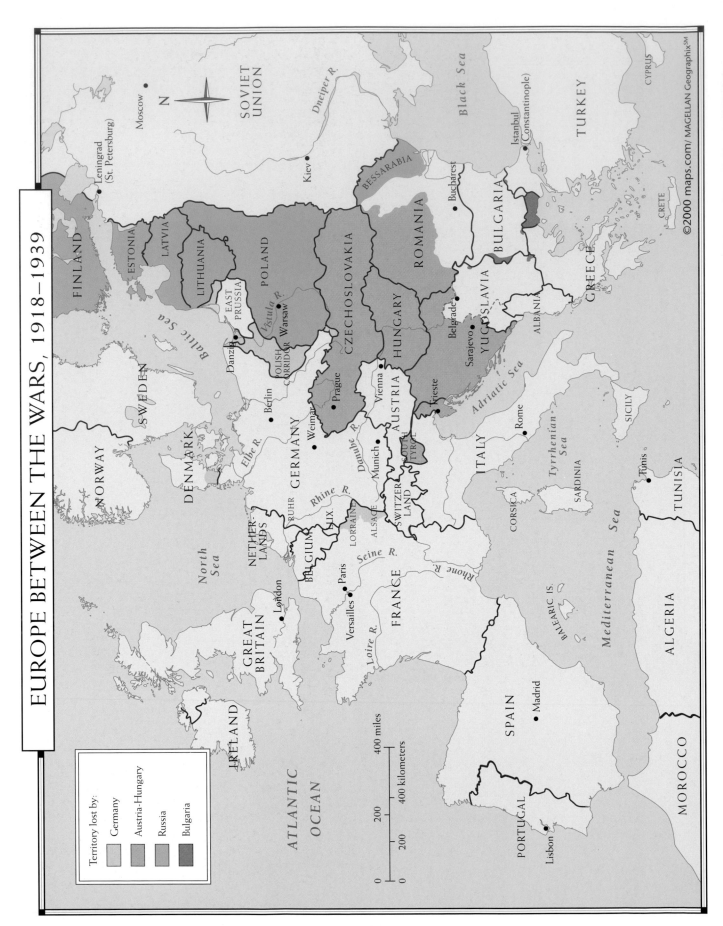

EUROPE BETWEEN THE WARS, 1918–1939

Territory lost by:
- Germany
- Austria-Hungary
- Russia
- Bulgaria

©2000 maps.com/ MAGELLAN Geographix℠

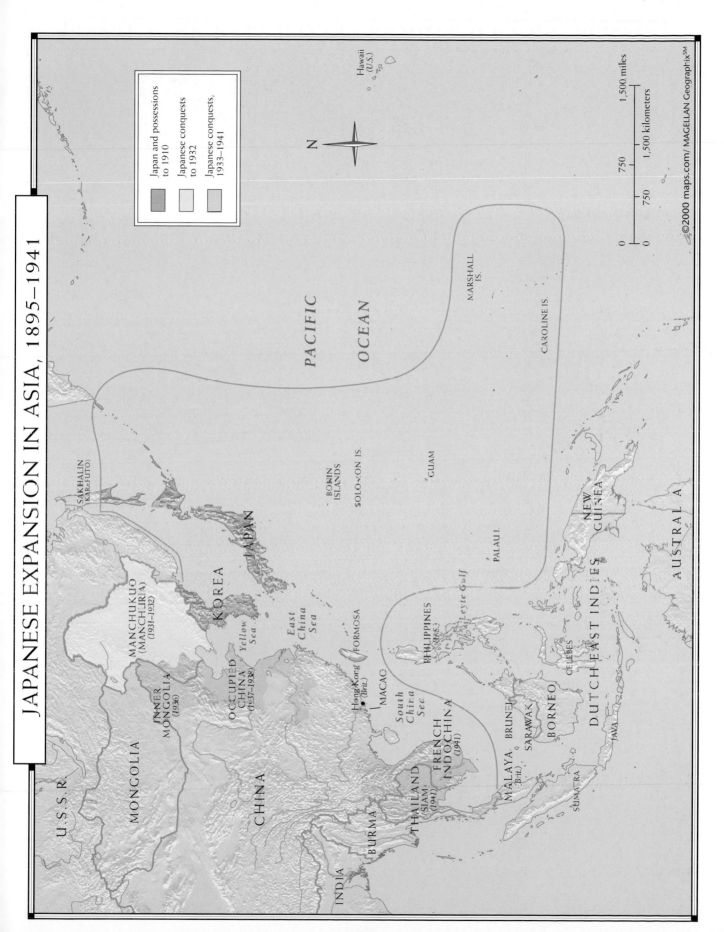

JAPANESE EXPANSION IN ASIA, 1895–1941

Legend:
- Japan and possessions to 1910
- Japanese conquests to 1932
- Japanese conquests, 1933–1941

N

1,500 miles
1,500 kilometers
0   750   750

©2000 maps.com/ MAGELLAN Geographix℠

Hawaii (U.S.)

PACIFIC OCEAN

MARSHALL IS.

CAROLINE IS.

SAKHALIN (KARAFUTO)

MONGOLIA

MANCHUKUO (MANCHURIA) (1931–1932)

INNER MONGOLIA (1936)

KOREA

JAPAN

Yellow Sea

East China Sea

OCCUPIED CHINA (1937–1938)

FORMOSA

BONIN ISLANDS

SOLOMON IS.

GUAM

PALAU I.

U.S.S.R.

CHINA

Hong Kong (Brit.)

MACAO

South China Sea

PHILIPPINES (U.S.)

Leyte Gulf

INDIA

BURMA

THAILAND SIAM (1941)

FRENCH INDOCHINA (1941)

MALAYA (Brit.)

BRUNEI

SARAWAK

BORNEO

CELEBES

DUTCH EAST INDIES

SUMATRA

JAVA

NEW GUINEA

AUSTRALIA

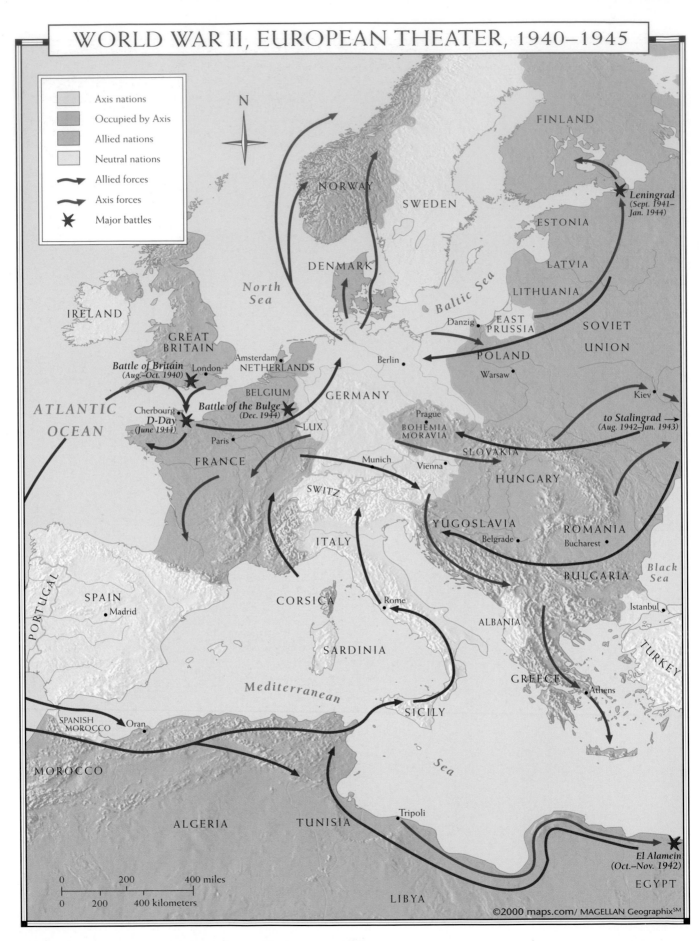

WORLD WAR II, EUROPEAN THEATER, 1940–1945

Legend:
- Axis nations
- Occupied by Axis
- Allied nations
- Neutral nations
- Allied forces
- Axis forces
- ★ Major battles

N

FINLAND

NORWAY

SWEDEN

ESTONIA

LATVIA

LITHUANIA

★ *Leningrad*
(Sept. 1941–Jan. 1944)

SOVIET UNION

DENMARK

Baltic Sea

Danzig

EAST PRUSSIA

POLAND

Warsaw

Berlin

North Sea

IRELAND

GREAT BRITAIN

Battle of Britain
(Aug.–Oct. 1940)

London

Amsterdam
NETHERLANDS

BELGIUM

GERMANY

Kiev

to Stalingrad
(Aug. 1942–Jan. 1943)

ATLANTIC OCEAN

Cherbourg

Battle of the Bulge
(Dec. 1944)

D-Day
(June 1944)

LUX.

Paris

FRANCE

Munich

Prague

BOHEMIA
MORAVIA

Vienna

SLOVAKIA

HUNGARY

SWITZ.

ITALY

YUGOSLAVIA

Belgrade

ROMANIA

Bucharest

Black Sea

PORTUGAL

SPAIN

Madrid

CORSICA

SARDINIA

Rome

BULGARIA

Istanbul

ALBANIA

TURKEY

Mediterranean

GREECE

Athens

Sea

SPANISH MOROCCO

Oran

SICILY

MOROCCO

ALGERIA

TUNISIA

Tripoli

Sea

El Alamein
(Oct.–Nov. 1942) ★

EGYPT

LIBYA

0   200   400 miles
0   200   400 kilometers

©2000 maps.com/ MAGELLAN Geographix℠

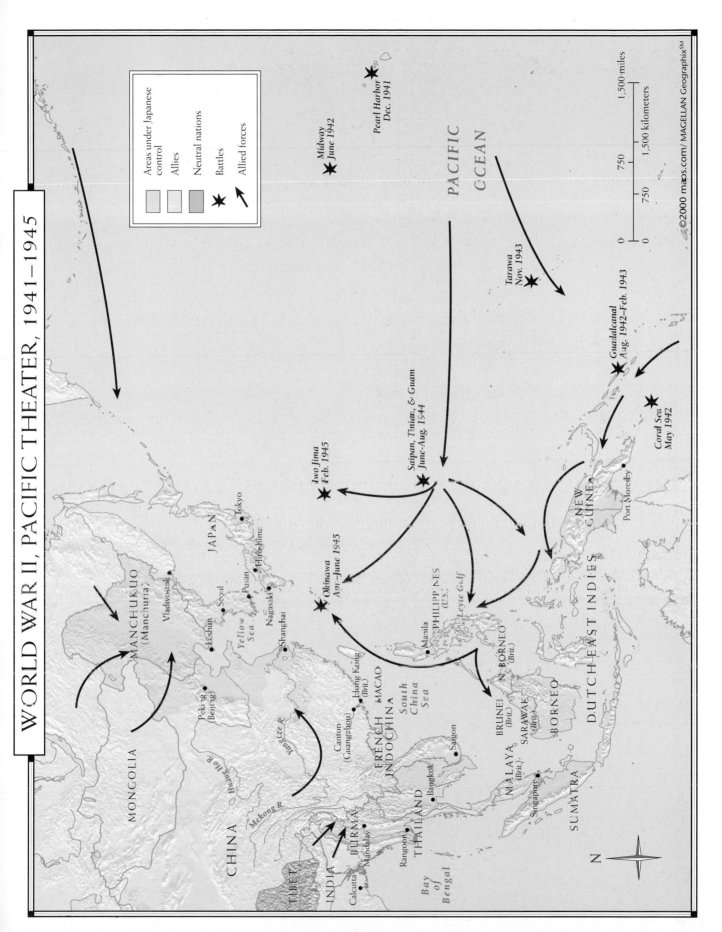

WORLD WAR II, PACIFIC THEATER, 1941–1945

Areas under Japanese control
Allies
Neutral nations
Battles
Allied forces

1,500 miles
1,500 kilometers
750
750
0

©2000 maps.com/ MAGELLAN Geographix℠

PACIFIC OCEAN

Pearl Harbor Dec. 1941
Midway June 1942
Tarawa Nov. 1943
Guadalcanal Aug. 1942–Feb. 1943
Coral Sea May 1942
Saipan, Tinian, & Guam June-Aug. 1944
Iwo Jima Feb. 1945
Okinawa Apr.–June 1945
Leyte Gulf
PHILIPPINES (U.S.)
NEW GUINEA
Port Moresby

MANCHUKUO (Manchuria)
MONGOLIA
CHINA
TIBET
INDIA
Calcutta
BURMA
Mandalay
Rangoon
THAILAND
Bangkok
FRENCH INDOCHINA
Saigon
MALAYA (Brit.)
Singapore
SUMATRA
DUTCH EAST INDIES
BORNEO
SARAWAK (Brit.)
BRUNEI (Brit.)
N. BORNEO (Brit.)
Manila
MACAO
Hong Kong (Brit.)
Canton (Guangzhou)
South China Sea
Peking (Beijing)
Shanghai
Yangtze R.
Huang Ho R.
Mekong R.
Bay of Bengal

JAPAN
Tokyo
Hiroshima
Nagasaki
Pusan
Seoul
Hushun
Vladivostok
Yellow Sea

N

— 41 —

INDEPENDENT STATES TO 1991

Legend:

- Gained independence between 1946–1959
- Independent prior to 1946
- Dependent states in 1990
- Independent after 1990
- Gained independence in the 1980s
- Gained independence in the 1970s
- Gained independence in the 1960s

ARCTIC OCEAN

PACIFIC OCEAN

NEW ZEALAND

PAPUA NEW GUINEA

AUSTRALIA

INDONESIA

PHILIPPINES

TAIWAN

JAPAN

N. KOREA

S. KOREA

BRUNEI

MALAYSIA

SINGAPORE

VIETNAM

LAOS

CAMBODIA

THAILAND

BURMA

BANG.

BHUTAN

NEPAL

INDIA

CHINA

MONGOLIA

RUSSIA

INDIAN OCEAN

MADAGASCAR

KAZAKHSTAN

UZBEKISTAN

KYRGYZSTAN

TAJIKISTAN

TURKMENISTAN

AFGHANISTAN

PAKISTAN

IRAN

OMAN

U.A.E.

QATAR

BAHRAIN

SAUDI ARABIA

KUWAIT

IRAQ

JORDAN

SYRIA

ISRAEL

LEB.

CYPRUS

TURKEY

ARMENIA

AZERBAIJAN

GEORGIA

YEMEN

DJIBOUTI

ERITREA

SOMALIA

ETHIOPIA

SUDAN

KENYA

UGANDA

RWANDA

BURUNDI

TANZANIA

MALAWI

ZAMBIA

ZIMBABWE

MOZAMBIQUE

SWAZILAND

LESOTHO

SOUTH AFRICA

BOTSWANA

NAMIBIA

ANGOLA

ZAIRE

CONGO

GABON

CAMEROON

C. A. R.

CHAD

NIGER

NIGERIA

BENIN

TOGO

GHANA

EQ. GUINEA

SAO TOME & PRINCIPE

BURKINA FASO

COTE D'IVOIRE

LIBERIA

SIERRA LEONE

GUINEA

GUINEA-BISSAU

GAMBIA

SENEGAL

MAURITANIA

MALI

WESTERN SAHARA (Mor.)

MOROCCO

ALGERIA

TUNISIA

LIBYA

EGYPT

NIGER

ESTONIA

LATVIA

LITHUANIA

BELARUS

UKRAINE

MOLDOVA

ROMANIA

BULGARIA

BOS.

CRO.

YUGO.-SER.

ALBANIA

GREECE

MACE.

HUNGARY

AUS.

SLOVAKIA

CZECH REP.

POLAND

GERMANY

NETH.

BEL.

LUX.

FRANCE

SWITZ.

ITALY

SLO.

SPAIN

PORTUGAL

GREAT BRITAIN

IRELAND

DENMARK

NORWAY

SWEDEN

FINLAND

ICELAND

GREENLAND (Den.)

NORTH ATLANTIC OCEAN

SOUTH ATLANTIC OCEAN

PACIFIC OCEAN

U.S.

CANADA

UNITED STATES

MEXICO

GUATEMALA

BELIZE

HONDURAS

EL SALVADOR

NICARAGUA

COSTA RICA

PANAMA

CUBA

JAMAICA

HAITI

DOMINICAN REPUBLIC

THE BAHAMAS

PUERTO RICO (U.S.)

TRINIDAD AND TOBAGO

COLOMBIA

VENEZUELA

GUYANA

SURINAME

FRENCH GUIANA (Fr.)

ECUADOR

PERU

BRAZIL

BOLIVIA

PARAGUAY

CHILE

ARGENTINA

URUGUAY

FALKLAND ISLANDS

N

©2000 maps.com/ MAGELLAN Geographix℠

COLD WAR EUROPE, 1946–1990

N

	NATO Alliance
	Warsaw Pact Nations

ICELAND

FINLAND

Helsinki • Leningrad

NORWAY
Oslo •

SWEDEN
Stockholm •

Riga •

North Sea

DENMARK
Copenhagen •

Vilnius •
Minsk •

SOVIET UNION

IRELAND
Dublin •

UNITED KINGDOM

NETHERLANDS
Amsterdam •

Elbe River

Berlin •
EAST GERMANY

Vistula R.

Warsaw •
POLAND

Kiev •

London •

Brussels •
BELGIUM
LUX.

Rhine R.
Bonn •
WEST GERMANY

Prague •
CZECHOSLOVAKIA

Paris •

Seine R.

Bratislava •
Danube River
Vienna •

Kishinev •

ATLANTIC OCEAN

Loire River

Munich •

AUSTRIA

Budapest •
HUNGARY

FRANCE

SWITZ.
Geneva •

ROMANIA

Po River

Belgrade •
YUGOSLAVIA
Sarajevo •

Bucharest •

BULGARIA
Sofia •

SPAIN
(Joined NATO in 1982)
Madrid •

Tiber R.

Rome •
ITALY

Skopje •

Tirana •
ALBANIA
(Withdrew from Warsaw Pact in 1968)

Istanbul •

TURKEY

PORTUGAL
Lisbon •

GREECE

Mediterranean Sea

Athens •

ALGERIA

| 0 | 200 | 400 miles |
| 0 | 200 | 400 kilometers |

THE VIETNAM WAR, 1964–1975

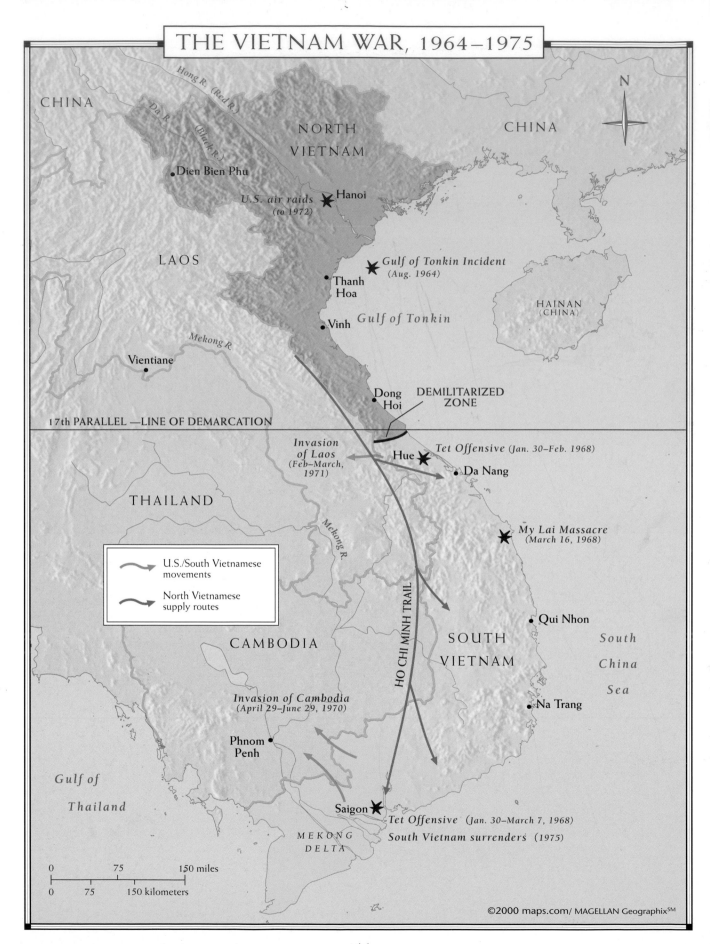

CHINA

NORTH VIETNAM

CHINA

N

Hong R. (Red R.)

Da R.

(Black R.)

Dien Bien Phu

U.S. air raids
(to 1972)

★ Hanoi

LAOS

★ *Gulf of Tonkin Incident*
(Aug. 1964)

Thanh Hoa

Gulf of Tonkin

HAINAN (CHINA)

Vinh

Mekong R.

Vientiane

Dong Hoi

DEMILITARIZED ZONE

17th PARALLEL —LINE OF DEMARCATION

Invasion of Laos
(Feb–March, 1971)

Hue ★ *Tet Offensive (Jan. 30–Feb. 1968)*

Da Nang

THAILAND

My Lai Massacre
(March 16, 1968)

Mekong R.

U.S./South Vietnamese movements

North Vietnamese supply routes

Qui Nhon

CAMBODIA

HO CHI MINH TRAIL

SOUTH VIETNAM

South China Sea

Invasion of Cambodia
(April 29–June 29, 1970)

Na Trang

Phnom Penh

Gulf of Thailand

Saigon ★

Tet Offensive (Jan. 30–March 7, 1968)

South Vietnam surrenders (1975)

MEKONG DELTA

| 0 | 75 | 150 miles |
| 0 | 75 | 150 kilometers |

STATES OF THE WORLD, 2000

Abbreviations legend:

AFGH. = Afghanistan
ALB. = Albania
ARM. = Armenia
AUS. = Austria
AZER. = Azerbaijan
BANG. = Bangladesh
BELA. = Belarus
BOS. & HERZ. = Bosnia and Herzegovina
BURK. FASO = Burkina Faso
BUL. = Bulgaria
CYP. = Cyprus

CAM. = Cameroon
CAMB. = Cambodia
C. AFR. REP. = Central African Republic
CRO. = Croatia
CZE. = Czech Republic
DEM. REP. OF THE CONGO = Democratic Republic of the Congo
DEN. = Denmark
EQ. GUINEA = Equatorial Guinea
EST. = Estonia
GER. = Germany
HOND. = Honduras

HUN. = Hungary
ISR. = Israel
KRYG. = Kyrgyzstan
LAT. = Latvia
LEB. = Lebanon
LITH. = Lithuania
LUX. = Luxemburg
MAC. = Macedonia
MOL. = Moldova
MYAN. = Myanmar
NETH. = Netherlands
POL. = Poland

ROM. = Romania
RUS. = Russia
SERB. = Serbia
SLO. = Slovakia
SLOV. = Slovenia
SWITZ. = Switzerland
SYR. = Syria
TAJIK. = Tajikstan
THAI. = Thailand
TURK. = Turkmenistan
UZBEK. = Uzbekistan
U.A.E. = United Arab Emirates

Pacific nations not shown on map:
FIJI, KIRIBATI, MARSHALL ISLANDS, PALAU, SAMOA, TONGA, TUVALU

Caribbean nations not labeled on map:
ANTIGUA & BARBUDA, ST KITTS & NEVIS ST. VINCENT & THE GRENADINES

European nations not labeled on map:
LIECHTENSTEIN, MONACO, SAN MARINO, VATICAN CITY

©2000 maps.com/ MAGELLAN Geographix℠

INDEX